SPORT PSYCHOLOGY

THE BASICS

Sport Psychology: The Basics provides an accessible introduction to the fundamental ideas at the heart of sport psychology today. It examines the links between sport participants' behaviours, their personality and their environment to identify the factors which affect performance. Exploring theory and practice, it uses case studies to illustrate how key areas of theory are applied within a sport psychologist's practice, answering such questions as:

- What is sport psychology and what do sport psychologists do?
- What factors affect sporting performance?
- Which psychological characteristics are associated with achievement in sport?
- How can performance be improved by using theory?

With a glossary of key terms, suggestions for further study and ideas for improving performance, *Sport Psychology: The Basics* is an ideal introduction for students of sport and coaches who would like to know more about how sport psychologists address questions about human behaviour in sport.

David Tod is Senior Lecturer in Psychology at the University of the Sunshine Coast, Australia.

The Basics

ACTING
BELLA MERLIN

AMERICAN PHILOSOPHY
NANCY STANLICK

ANCIENT NEAR EAST
DANIEL C. SNELL

ANTHROPOLOGY
PETER METCALF

ARCHAEOLOGY (SECOND EDITION)
CLIVE GAMBLE

ART HISTORY
GRANT POOKE AND DIANA NEWALL

ARTIFICIAL INTELLIGENCE
KEVIN WARWICK

THE BIBLE
JOHN BARTON

BIOETHICS
ALASTAIR V. CAMPBELL

BUDDHISM
CATHY CANTWELL

THE CITY
KEVIN ARCHER

CONTEMPORARY LITERATURE
SUMAN GUPTA

CRIMINAL LAW
JONATHAN HERRING

CRIMINOLOGY (SECOND EDITION)
SANDRA WALKLATE

DANCE STUDIES
JO BUTTERWORTH

EASTERN PHILOSOPHY
VICTORIA S. HARRISON

ECONOMICS (SECOND EDITION)
TONY CLEAVER

EDUCATION
KAY WOOD

ENERGY
MICHAEL SCHOBERT

EUROPEAN UNION (SECOND EDITION)
ALEX WARLEIGH-LACK

EVOLUTION
SHERRIE LYONS

FILM STUDIES (SECOND EDITION)
AMY VILLAREJO

FINANCE (SECOND EDITION)
ERIK BANKS

FREE WILL
MEGHAN GRIFFITH

GENDER
HILARY LIPS

GLOBAL MIGRATION
BERNADETTE HANLON AND THOMAS VICINIO

HUMAN GENETICS
RICKI LEWIS

HUMAN GEOGRAPHY
ANDREW JONES

INTERNATIONAL RELATIONS
PETER SUTCH AND JUANITA ELIAS

ISLAM (SECOND EDITION)
COLIN TURNER

JOURNALISM STUDIES
MARTIN CONBOY

JUDAISM
JACOB NEUSNER

LANGUAGE (SECOND EDITION)
R.L. TRASK

SPORT PSYCHOLOGY
THE BASICS

David Tod

Routledge
Taylor & Francis Group

LONDON AND NEW YORK

First published 2014
by Routledge
2 Park Square, Milton Park, Abingdon, Oxon OX14 4RN

and by Routledge
711 Third Avenue, New York, NY 10017

Routledge is an imprint of the Taylor & Francis Group, an informa business

© 2014 David Tod

British Library Cataloguing in Publication Data
A catalogue record for this book is available from the British Library

Library of Congress Cataloging in Publication Data
Tod, David.
Sport psychology: the basics / David Tod.
pages cm.—(The basics)
Includes bibliographical references and index.
1. Sports—Psychological aspects. I. Title.
GV706.4.T643 2014
796.01'9—dc23
2013046596

ISBN: 978-0-415-83449-0 (hbk)
ISBN: 978-0-415-83450-6 (pbk)
ISBN: 978-1-315-77442-8 (ebk)

Typeset in Bembo
by Book Now Ltd, London

Printed and bound in the United States of America
by Edwards Brothers Malloy on sustainably sourced paper

CONTENTS

ILLUSTRATIONS

FIGURES

TABLES

BOXES

INTRODUCTION

CHAPTER LEARNING OBJECTIVES

1 Define sport psychology.
2 Outline the difference between sport psychology and exercise psychology.
3 Detail sport psychology as an academic field and as an applied profession.
4 Demonstrate why sport psychology is an applied science.
5 Show how non-sport psychologists can use sport psychology knowledge.
6 Detail the typical training involved in becoming a sport psychologist.

Buffy plays for Sunnydale high school's female basketball team, and she is about to step up to the free throw line during the final seconds of a closely fought game against a local school with which her team shares a fierce rivalry. Her two points will win the contest. She has been having a terrible year, however, having returned from a knee injury that forced a premature end to her previous season. Buffy started the previous season strongly, and she had felt like the hoop was so large she could have scored with a fitness ball. Since her injury, Buffy has been hesitant in all facets of the game and plagued by self-doubts. Her coach, Giles, realises he needs to call a timeout to help Buffy, but is unsure what to say. Take a minute to think what you would say if you were the team's sport psychologist.

Giles' situation with Buffy illustrates some issues that fall within the scope of sport psychology. Most individuals would offer Giles an opinion that would echo psychological themes, such as telling Buffy to relax, take a deep breath, think positively, or focus on the task. These opinions reveal that most people have some familiarity with psychological ideas, and that is one reason why sport psychology is a fascinating discipline: most athletes, coaches and sports fans can engage and contribute meaningfully to a conversation on the topic. Given that many people have some understanding of psychological knowledge, be it from a lay or academic perspective, you might find some information presented in this book familiar. Sport psychologists study psychological phenomena scientifically to separate valid explanations from those not supported by evidence. Doing so provides knowledge and strategies that can help individuals improve their performances or gain satisfaction and happiness from their sporting participation. In this chapter I define sport psychology, detail its scope, show how it is different from related subjects, describe why it is an applied science, demonstrate how interested people can use sport psychology knowledge, and discuss the training involved in becoming a sport psychologist.

SPORT PSYCHOLOGY DEFINED

Sport psychology is often defined as the study of behaviour in sport. More broadly, the field is a scientific discipline focused on examining how thoughts, feelings, behaviour and environmental factors interact. Sport psychologists strive to describe, explain, predict and perhaps change people's thoughts, feelings and behaviour in sporting contexts so they can enjoy their participation more, enhance their performance, or achieve other benefits, such as stress reduction or an increased sense of well-being. In scenarios similar to the one above involving Buffy at the free throw line, for example, sport psychologists may start by observing and describing the situation: what thoughts typically go through athletes' heads when they experience pressure? What feelings do they experience? How do they often behave? What environmental factors seem to influence them? After describing these types of situations, sport psychologists aim to offer an explanation that could account for their observations. Perhaps injuries lower athletes' confidence and increase their self-doubts, leading to anxieties and tension. Their increased anxieties and tension may then affect their abilities to make decisions automatically and move in a coordinated fashion. Finally, their interrupted thoughts and movement patterns may hinder their performance outcomes, such as their lowered success rates at the free throw line. Sport psychologists then test their explanations to find out if they can predict behaviour and performance. Having found evidence that they can predict outcomes, sport psychologists might develop and test ways to change athletes' thoughts, feelings, behaviours or environments to increase performance and enjoyment. If successful, then sport psychologists have developed scientifically supported strategies for helping clients. These strategies could be used to help Buffy above. Based on current sport psychology knowledge and practice, for example, if increased anxiety and tension seem to be interfering with Buffy's performance, a sport psychologist may teach her a relaxation technique to reduce tension and a self-talk cue to direct her attention to helpful thoughts.

Building on the definition just presented, a number of sport psychologists have noted that the discipline has two broad foci (Williams and Straub 2010):

1 How do psychological factors influence behaviour and performance in sport?
2 What are the psychological effects of participation in sport?

Examples of specific questions subsumed under the first focus include:

- Will psychological strategies, such as relaxation and self-talk, help Buffy focus her attention on the task at hand, stay relaxed and perform well?
- Do people's anxieties about their bodies cause them to socialise less with teammates or even withdraw from sport?
- Do sprinters' levels of self-confidence influence their race times?

Answers to these types of questions allow sport psychologists to find ways to help athletes achieve their goals and gain happiness from their participation in sport.

Examples of specific questions covered by the second broad focus include:

- How will Buffy's success or failure at the free throw line influence her self-esteem?
- Can participating in team sports teach people how to work in groups and leadership skills?
- Does sport build character?

Answers to these types of questions help sport psychologists (and others) debate the value of sport for individuals and communities. A common justification for spending public money on sport is the proposed psychological and social benefits that athletes and societies accrue from taking part (for example, much rhetoric surrounding the justification countries give for bidding to host major sporting events, like the Olympics, involves the psychological benefits for its citizens). Sport psychologists are equipped to examine whether these claims are plausible.

Sport psychology has been influenced by several established fields of inquiry, with the two main ones being (a) sport and exercise science (which was typically labelled Physical Education or Kinesiology when sport psychology emerged in earnest during the sixties) and (b) psychology. Both sport and exercise science and psychology are broad subject areas with many sub-disciplines, as Table I.1 illustrates. Sport psychology has been influenced by each of the sub-disciplines in Table I.1, along with others, in its quest to examine athletes' thoughts, feelings and behaviours. Well-trained sport psychologists will understand the basic principles in each of these related sub-disciplines.

It may not be immediately apparent why effective sport psychologists understand the basic principles of various disciplines outside the field. Most professionals, however, realise psychological factors interact with other variables to influence performance. For example, researchers have shown that self-talk (a psychological factor referring to the words that athletes say to themselves) and anxiety influences movement kinematics and kinetics to affect performance (Collins

Table I.1: Example psychology and sport and exercise science sub-disciplines from which sport psychology draws

Psychology	Sport and exercise science
Counselling psychology	Biomechanics
Clinical psychology	Exercise physiology
Developmental psychology	Motor learning
Health psychology	Coaching science
Individual differences	Sports medicine
Psychophysiology	Sport sociology
Organisational psychology	Sport pedagogy
Abnormal psychology	

et al. 2001; Tod *et al.* 2009). Self-talk (e.g. 'jump high') might increase a volleyball player's jump height. Anxiety might disrupt a walker's technique. Understanding how psychological factors interact with other variables leads to a greater understanding of behaviour in sport than if these factors were studied in isolation.

DIFFERENCES BETWEEN SPORT PSYCHOLOGY AND EXERCISE PSYCHOLOGY

For many years professionals considered sport and exercise psychology to be a single field in which psychological principles were applied to competitive sport, physical activity and exercise domains. As the field has developed, professionals have been able to specialise, studying topics and offering academic courses focused on either sport or exercise. It has become increasingly difficult for academics to appreciate the breadth of, and stay current with, the psychological knowledge associated with both sport and exercise. The two fields have diverged and evolved towards different emphases. Whereas sport psychology addresses thoughts, feelings and behaviours in competitive sporting contexts, exercise psychology focuses on physical activity, exercise and health domains.

The split is not complete; in many universities, sport and exercise psychology is still taught under the one title. Professional organisations around the globe offering registration or licencing schemes may require practitioners to have knowledge and skills relevant to both domains. The emergence of two fields is most visible in places, such as universities and elite sporting institutes, where professionals have focused on specific types of people (e.g. helping athletes enhance their competitive results or finding ways to increase activity levels in the general population). Outside of these environments, such as for psychologists in private practice or professionals working with sub-elite athletes, the differences are less noticeable, because practitioners may need to help a variety of people.

SPORT PSYCHOLOGY AS AN ACADEMIC FIELD AND AS AN APPLIED PROFESSION

As an academic field, professionals focus primarily on creating and disseminating sport psychology knowledge and they are normally employed in universities. When undertaking research or creating knowledge, professionals apply scientific methods to examine psychological phenomena within sport. Their objective is to develop and test theories that explain the principles underlying the interactions between athletes and their environments. For example, a number of experiments have been conducted to find out if psychological strategies can help strength athletes (weightlifters, bodybuilders, American footballers and rugby union players; Tod *et al.* 2003) mentally prepare during their resistance training sessions and increase their displays of strength. These studies might then lead to strategies for helping athletes.

Once researchers have identified answers to specific questions, they then disseminate that knowledge to others in numerous ways. One way professionals inform others about their research is through the publication of articles in professional and scientific journals. There are, for example, several scientific journals focused on sport psychology, such as the *Journal of Sport & Exercise Psychology*[1] and *Psychology of Sport and Exercise.*[2] Investigators may also present their work at conferences held by organisations, including the Association for Applied Sport Psychology[3] and the Fédération Européenne de Psychologie des Sports et des Activités Corporelles (FEPSAC, European Federation of Sport Psychology).[4]

Within the academic realm, professionals may also teach students and others sport psychology knowledge as part of psychology or sport and exercise science-based qualifications at both the undergraduate and postgraduate levels. In some countries, sport psychology may also form part of the high-school physical education or psychology curriculum. For example, in many under-graduate sport science or kinesiology degrees, educators may offer courses introducing students to applied sport psychology knowledge focused on ways to help athletes enhance performance. These students may desire to become applied practitioners who work with athletes, coaches, teams and sporting organisations.

When working as applied professionals, practitioners apply sport psychology knowledge to assist athletes and coaches in resolving their issues, achieving their goals and enhancing performance. For example, practitioners may draw on Locke and Latham's (2002) influential goal-setting theory to help athletes plan and achieve their sporting dreams. In recent years a number of professional organisations around the globe have developed registration, accreditation, or licensing schemes so that practitioners can demonstrate to potential clients that they have the knowledge and skills to be effective. In the USA, for example, the Association for Applied Sport Psychology certifies individuals as 'certified consultants'. In the UK, for example, the Health and Care Professions Council[5] registers individuals as 'sport and exercise psychologists'.

Some people have suggested that legally sanctioned and other accreditation, registration, or licensing schemes imply there is a demand for practitioners and newly qualified professionals can expect to make a full-time income from working with athletes. Although some people do make a full-time living as practitioners, the limited evidence suggests the majority of people working in the field with athletes do so part-time and derive the majority of their incomes from other sources, such as teaching at universities or working as psychologists or counsellors in other domains (e.g. education or health settings; Meyers *et al.* 2001). Also, most individuals completing applied sport psychology courses do not become applied practitioners (Williams and Scherzer 2003). The data from these studies, however, were largely gathered in the late 1990s and were confined mostly to the USA: the employment landscape may have changed, rendering this information obsolete. It is possible to make a living from applied sport psychology work, although initially at least, it may be prudent for people contemplating such a career to consider how they might be able to diversify their income until they have built their client base. Two typical ways most individuals do so is by completing a PhD and becoming an academic or becoming practitioner psychologists in other domains (e.g. clinical, education, occupational).

The popular and news media tend to focus on the highest levels of sport, so it is understandable that many individuals believe that sport psychology only applies to elite athletes and typically when they are in a crisis and performing poorly. Such coverage contributes to an inaccurate view of professionals as purveyors of quick fixes or 'band aid psychology'. Although elite athletes do benefit from sport psychology knowledge, they do not need to be performing poorly or be in crisis to get assistance. They are also not the only beneficiaries of psychological assistance. The majority of athletes, coaches, or other people involved in sport may gain from an applied sport psychologist's help. Youth, senior, sub-elite, able-bodied, disabled, female and male athletes can all benefit, and sport psychologists can also help these individuals prepare for and reflect on, as well as cope with performance. Athletes and coaches also experience difficulties outside of the sporting context, such as relationship breakdowns, mental health issues or substance abuse, and well-trained sport psychologists can assist them with these issues. In addition, suitably qualified practitioners understand how these difficulties may be influenced by, or may hinder, sporting performance and participation.

THE SCIENTIFIC BASIS OF SPORT PSYCHOLOGY

Effective training to become a sport psychologist is based on the scientist-practitioner model. In this approach to education, students are trained to adhere to the scientific principles of problem-solving and to base decisions when working with clients on the best evidence available within humane and ethical boundaries. For example, practitioners are encouraged by professional organisations to develop the competencies and skills known to help clients, and to apply only those interventions for which there is evidence that they assist people. It is also hoped that students trained within the scientist-practitioner framework will contribute to the evidence basis of the discipline throughout their careers, through means such as constructing case studies and undertaking research they then share with their colleagues. Adherence to the scientific basis of sport psychology is a core value to many sport psychologists because it helps demonstrate that they are professionals capable of offering specialised help to clients and that their services are approved by relevant credible organisations, such as State Licencing Boards in the USA or the Health and Care Professions Council in the UK.

To be effective scientist-practitioners, students receive training in the scientific method. The scientific method is an approach to solving problems, answering specific questions, and learning about the world in which we live. It is based on the accumulation of observable and repeatable evidence which informs theory development. A theory is a model that integrates a series of facts or observations about the world. In sport psychology, theories may be broad and applicable to much behaviour or they may be more specific in scope. Social learning theory, developed by the highly influential psychologist, Albert Bandura (1977), is an example of a theory that helps explain much behaviour in sport. According to social learning theory, athletes learn acceptable and unacceptable behaviour via reward, punishment and modelling (watching how other people act). The theory further suggests that people learn most of their complicated behaviours from modelling rather than direct reward and punishment. For example, in some sports, children may learn that it is acceptable to verbally abuse the opposition, or engage in trash talk (or sledging), because they see professional or elite athletes doing so and being praised for being aggressive and competitive. In other sports, children may learn that such behaviour is not acceptable because elite athletes are penalised for such unsporting behaviour. Goal-setting theory is much narrower in scope than social learning theory, but has been helpful in understanding how athletes may best use the strategy to achieve their dreams.

Given the complexity of behaviour in sport and the various factors that influence how athletes act and perform, it may be difficult for practitioners to make informed decisions without drawing on a suitable theory. A good theory helps sport psychologists ask relevant questions when working with clients and use the assessment tools that will allow them to understand athletes' issues. Further, a good theory will then guide practitioners' decision-making towards those answers and interventions with the best chance of helping clients resolve their issues and achieve their aims.

The scientific method may be illustrated in a four-step process, as presented in Figure I.1 (Thomas *et al.* 2011). To start the

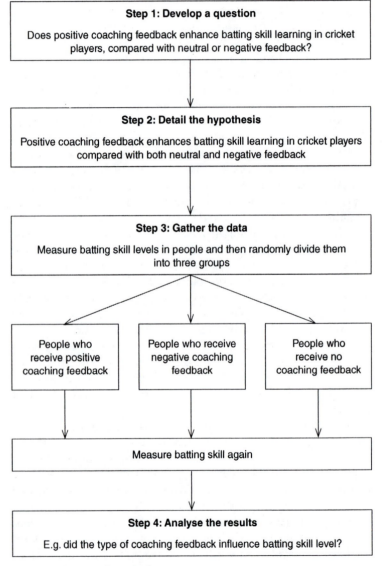

Figure I.1: The scientific method.

process, sport psychology researchers develop a specific question to answer, such as the influence of positive coaching feedback on cricketers' acquisition of batting technique. In developing their studies, scientists will review existing research to find out if their questions have already been answered and will talk with athletes and coaches to identify those they consider worthwhile answering. Once suitable questions have been developed, sport psychologists will determine the best ways of defining and measuring the variables or factors in which they are interested. In the cricket example, researchers will need to define positive coaching feedback and determine how they will measure batting skill acquisition.

In step 2, scientists describe their hypotheses or their expected results. Most likely in the cricket example, researchers might expect that positive coaching feedback is associated with better batting skill acquisition compared with neutral, negative, or no coaching feedback. Researchers may develop their hypotheses from learning about the results from existing research or from conversations with coaches and athletes. Having developed a series of specific hypotheses, sport psychology scientists can then develop high-quality studies to answer their questions. There are different types of studies that scientists undertake and they range in the quality of evidence provided to answer the question. Box I.1 details examples of the different studies sport psychology researchers often undertake, ranging from meta-analyses and experiments (that provide the highest quality evidence) to case studies and expert opinion (which are generally considered to yield lower quality evidence). In the current cricket example, researchers will probably aim to conduct an experiment and randomly allocate novice cricketers to groups that receive different types of coaching feedback (e.g. positive, neutral or negative feedback). The researchers might measure the cricketers' batting skill levels before and after they are given feedback. The scientists will probably attempt to standardise the feedback as much as possible (amount, frequency, delivery, etc.), so that the only difference between the groups is whether it is positive, negative or neutral. They may also standardise the type of cricketers they include in the study (gender, age, etc.) so

BOX I.1: **LEVELS OF EVIDENCE**

- Meta-analysis: A study in which investigators use statistical procedures to combine the results of all the research that has been conducted on a topic to determine a relationship between two variables, such as confidence and performance. When a meta-analysis combines the results of a large number of well-designed experiments, then it is considered to be the strongest form of scientific evidence.
- Experiment: An investigation in which researchers manipulate one variable (independent variable; e.g., coaching strategy) to observe its effect on another variable (dependent variable; e.g., learning). When well-designed and any other possible influencing factor is controlled, an experiment allows researchers to say the independent variable caused the dependent variable to change (e.g., good coaching allowed athletes to learn a new skill).
- Longitudinal/cohort study: A piece of research in which investigators follow a group of people over time, measuring variables on multiple occasions. If the researchers manipulate an independent variable to observe its effect on a dependent variable, then it is a longitudinal experiment, otherwise it is considered a descriptive study.
- Cross-sectional quantitative descriptive study: An investigation in which researchers measure variables using numbers, such as scores on a personality questionnaire. The investigators do not manipulate any variables, but may try as much as possible to observe them in their natural environment. Although typically easier to undertake than an experiment, it is not normally possible to infer causality or conclude that one variable influenced another.
- Cross-sectional qualitative descriptive study: A piece of research in which investigators explore people's experiences, perceptions and knowledge in-depth using words, text, pictures, videos, etc. as data. The results are based on researchers' subjective interpretations of the data. Although such studies may provide a rich understanding of the topic, they can be time-consuming, labour intensive and open to researcher bias.
- Case study: An in-depth investigation of a single person, event, organisation, etc. It is not normally possible to establish a causal relationship between two variables or to generalise to other similar athletes, events, organisations, etc.

- Expert opinion: Evidence based on the opinion of a person considered to be knowledgeable about the topic. Experts may be biased in their thinking and unreliable. Generally considered the lowest level of evidence.

Understanding the levels of evidence helps people judge the robustness of knowledge. Knowing, for example, that the evidence for an intervention's effectiveness was based on a meta-analysis, leads to greater confidence in the strategy than if the data had been generated from a case study.

that factors that might interact with feedback are controlled. Perhaps, for example, experienced batters respond differently to feedback compared with novice players. Having developed a high-quality study, researchers then engage in step 3 when they collect the data.

In step 4, researchers will analyse the data. In the cricket example, the researchers will probably measure skill level numerically and use a statistical test to answer the question: does positive coaching feedback enhance batting skill acquisition compared with neutral or negative feedback? Scientists will then attempt to interpret the results, such as suggesting how the findings might help coaches or offering an explanation for what they observed. If the results indicated that positive coaching feedback led to greater skill acquisition compared with negative feedback, for example, the scientists may suggest it was because the athletes had greater confidence in their ability. The researchers may also recommend that coaches give positive rather than negative feedback.

Having completed the process, scientists then want to tell others about their study. Disseminating results allows athletes and coaches learn how they might enhance their performance or gain greater happiness from their participation. Also, other researchers can design new studies to extend the results. For example, other researchers might conduct another study to find out if increased confidence was the reason that positive feedback led to increased skill-learning.

HOW NON-SPORT PSYCHOLOGISTS CAN USE SPORT PSYCHOLOGY KNOWLEDGE

The scientific method is a problem-solving process and can be used by any athlete, coach or sport-related individual in similar ways to researchers to help them apply sport psychology knowledge to their specific situation. Such application can be realised through self-reflection and experimentation. As an example, a football trainer may have difficulty encouraging team players to undertake extra training outside of squad sessions. To help her solve her problem, she reads a sport psychology textbook about motivation and ways to change behaviour. As the trainer reads the text she may identify ways she could apply the information. The trainer could then implement her ideas and keep a record of how much extra conditioning the players undertook. After some time, the trainer will have the information she needs to decide if her strategies worked and whether to continue or change her approach. Most likely, not every strategy the trainer used will help each athlete in the squad, and she may be more successful in modifying behaviour if she is adaptable and changes strategies to suit specific players. With reflection and experimentation, she will increase the probability that she will identify what works best in her situation.

TRAINING FOR A CAREER IN SPORT PSYCHOLOGY

Working as an applied practitioner, teacher or scientist in sport psychology can be rewarding. Assisting athletes to improve their performance, to resolve their issues, or to gain greater meaning from their sport can be highly satisfying. Contributing to the knowledge base or finding evidence for a novel intervention is also fulfilling. Equally, helping students to develop themselves and progress towards completing a qualification may leave teachers with a sense of making a difference in people's lives. Such personal reward is in addition to the pleasure of working in a sport-related industry. Sport participation can be enjoyable and beneficial mentally, physically and socially, and is highly valued by large segments of the population in many societies. It is understandable then that students and others are attracted to sport psychology. A common question is, what qualifications are needed to operate as a sport psychologist?

The answer to that question varies depending on the country in which the individual wishes to work. In many countries there are no government sanctioned criteria or professional standards that need to be observed. In these places, anybody can work professionally in a sport-psychology-related job if they can convince somebody to pay them. Increasingly around the globe, however, organisations have developed recommended or mandatory educational pathways that need to be completed to be eligible to gain official professional recognition. In addition, there may be legislation detailing the titles by which people may advertise themselves. In the USA, for example, the word 'psychologist' is a protected title. Only licensed psychologists may promote themselves as 'sport psychologists'. In the UK, only those individuals registered by the Health and Care Professions Council may use the title 'sport and exercise psychologist' or derivative (e.g. 'sport psychologist'). An initial starting point for people interested in securing sport-psychology-related employment is to find out what criteria and standards apply in their country.

In several countries, such as Australia and the UK, training to be a professionally recognised practitioner typically includes undergraduate and postgraduate study in psychology, with complementary tuition in sport science. In these countries, students who have achieved an undergraduate degree in sport science may find they have to start again, unless they have also completed sufficient study in psychology. Specialisation as a practitioner normally begins in earnest at the postgraduate level. Psychology study at the undergraduate level is typically theoretical and covers a wide range of topics, including several of those listed under the psychology heading in Table I.1. Unless there is a lecturer teaching on the psychology programme with a specific interest in sport, there may be no sport psychology modules at the undergraduate level. At the postgraduate level, students usually complete: (a) knowledge-based modules on sport psychology (and usually exercise psychology), along with a selection of other psychology, sport science and/or research methods courses; (b) a research dissertation; and (c) supervised work experience where they start helping athletes under the guidance of a qualified mentor. These activities may lead to master's degrees or professional doctorates. Again the specifics are generally influenced by the county's relevant professional bodies.

Even with the development of educational pathways and professional standards in many countries, there exist individuals who have no qualifications in those territories who offer applied sport psychology services to athletes, coaches and teams. These people may use various titles to describe themselves as 'mental coaches', 'mental skill trainers', 'performance consultants', etc. (qualified practitioners may also advertise themselves by different titles because the word 'psychologist' may be off-putting to some athletes and coaches). It would be inaccurate to assume that practitioners without professionally recognised qualifications will be ineffective in helping athletes. Some of these individuals may provide excellent services, whereas others may be less effective and leave behind a distaste and distrust of sport psychology. Equally, having professional qualifications does not guarantee the person will be an effective practitioner. Even qualified individuals may give applied sport psychology a poor reputation and may be incompetent or unfit to work. Professional qualifications do, however, reassure consumers (athletes and coaches) that professionals have been judged by their peers as having the competencies prescribed as necessary for being an effective practitioner.

In contrast, becoming an academic most often relies on the achievement of a PhD, and demonstrating a capacity to obtain research funding, produce research and teach. In places such as the UK, Australia and New Zealand, a PhD consists of a 3-year programme of research in which the student undertakes a number of studies (often three or four depending on their size) and submits a thesis. In other areas, such as North America, PhDs consist of a mixture of conducting research and completing advanced courses in the area. There is typically no requirement for an academic to engage in applied work with athletes, although many do because of their passion for helping people. Although traditionally, qualifications leading to practitioner status were not needed to become an academic, in recent years, people with such professional credentials offer the added benefit to universities of being able to mentor students undertaking supervised work experience.

Bringing these ideas together, individuals wishing to pursue careers in sport psychology would find it beneficial to acquaint themselves with the legal and professional requirements in the countries where they hope to work. It would also be salubrious for them to consider if they want to be an applied sport psychologist or a researcher before planning their training. Nevertheless, completing both a PhD and the requirements to obtain professional recognition ensures that students are best prepared for their careers.

CONCLUSION

When listening to athletes and coaches being interviewed after they have won or lost an event, you will typically find that they offer psychology-related explanations for their performances. After winning an event a team captain may praise the players for maintaining focus or staying cool under pressure. After a loss the captain may suggest the players performed as individuals and didn't work as a team, or indicate the opposition had a greater desire to win. These explanations are then discussed and debated by journalists, spectators and sport psychologists. Sport psychologists adopt a rigorous and scientific perspective in their attempts to understand athletes' behaviours, thoughts, feelings and performances. The application of the scientific perspective has yielded a body of knowledge that forms the foundation of the discipline. As applied scientist-practitioners, sport psychologists aim to then use the knowledge created to help athletes and others achieve their sporting goals, enhance their performance and gain greater levels of happiness and satisfaction in their participation. In the following chapters I will present the basic principles underpinning sport psychology knowledge before addressing ways practitioners apply that knowledge to the benefit of sport participants.

NOTES

1 http://journals.humankinetics.com/jsep.
2 http://www.journals.elsevier.com/psychology-of-sport-and-exercise.
3 http://www.appliedsportpsych.org.
4 http://www.fepsac.com.
5 http://www.hpc-uk.org.

REFERENCES

Bandura, A. (1977). *Social learning theory*. Englewood Cliffs, NJ: Prentice Hall.

Collins, D., Jones, B., Fairweather, M., Doolan, S. and Priestley, N. (2001). Examining anxiety associated changes in movement patterns. *International Journal of Sport Psychology, 32*, 223–242.

Locke, E. A. and Latham, G. P. (2002). Building a practically useful theory of goal setting and task motivation: A 35-year odyssey. *American Psychologist, 57*, 705–717.

Meyers, A. W., Coleman, J. K., Whelan, J. P. and Mehlenbeck, R. S. (2001). Examining careers in sport psychology: Who is working and who is making money? *Professional Psychology: Research and Practice, 32*, 5–11.

Thomas, J. R., Nelson, J. K. and Silverman, S. J. (2011). *Research methods in physical activity* (6th ed.). Champaign, IL: Human Kinetics.

Tod, D., Iredale, F. and Gill, N. (2003). 'Psyching-up' and muscular force production. *Sport Medicine, 33*, 47–58.

Tod, D., Thatcher, R., McGuigan, M. and Thatcher, J. (2009). Effects of instructional and motivational self-talk on the vertical jump. *Journal of Strength and Conditioning Research, 23*, 196–202.

Williams, J. M. and Scherzer, C. B. (2003). Tracking the training and careers of graduates of advanced degree programs in sport psychology, 1994 to 1999. *Journal of Applied Sport Psychology, 15*, 335–353.

Williams, J. M. and Straub, W. F. (2010). Sport psychology: Past, present, future. In J. M. Williams (Ed.), *Applied sport psychology: Personal growth to peak performance* (pp. 1–17). Boston: McGraw Hill.

PERSONALITY

Like his brother Dean, when Sam enrolled at the University of Kansas he decided to trial for the men's rugby union team. And like Dean, Sam enjoyed the game and demonstrated flair for the sport. He quickly became a starting player and in his first year was awarded 'most valuable player' after four games. Sam wondered if he could eventually get into the US national team. The thought of representing his country appealed to Sam, but he was unsure if such an ambition was realistic. One Saturday, after beating the Kansas City Blues team, Sam approached Coach Bobby Singer in the team's club house above Johnny's Tavern and asked if it was realistic to aim to play for the United States. Coach thought a moment before saying yes, it was possible, and he probably had a better chance than Dean had when he had been playing. Coach said Dean had also been a great player, but Sam was likely to be better, because he had the character to develop his skills and was hungrier for success. He also thought Sam applied himself more to training, whereas Dean had been happy to enjoy the social life that surrounded the team. Compared with Dean, Sam also took more responsibility for his weaknesses, was more coachable, was a better team player and was more ambitious.

Like Coach Singer, many people believe that personality factors contribute to sporting success. As athletes move up the sporting pyramid and participate at elite levels of competition they become increasingly similar to each other physically. Many individuals also suggest elite athletes share similar personality characteristics, such as being driven, having high pain thresholds and possessing unshakeable self-confidence. When sport psychology was establishing itself as an academic discipline in the 1960s and 70s, personality was a popular topic and researchers published more than 1,000 studies examining if specific personality traits, such as extraversion, could predict sporting performance (Fisher, 1984). In this chapter I define personality, explain how sport psychologists view and assess the construct, and summarise research examining its relationship with sport performance.

PERSONALITY DEFINED

When discussing what constitutes personality, most people will typically suggest that it includes the characteristics that make people different from each other, echoing common psychological definitions. Personality refers to the collection of enduring psychological features that makes individuals different from others. This definition contains three ideas:

1 Personality includes the sum of our social, perceptual, cognitive, affective and behavioural tendencies.
2 Although people may share some features, the blend of their characteristics makes them unique.
3 Psychologists typically assume some consistency to personality and behaviour.

The unique blend of enduring psychological tendencies is one reason why understanding personality helps sports psychologists and others, such as coaches, perform their jobs well. Learning about athletes' personalities and getting to know them as individuals allow sport psychologists (and others) to decide how to deal with and help them most effectively. Coach Singer, for example, would likely treat Sam and Dean differently to get the best out of them because of their different personalities.

APPROACHES TO PERSONALITY

As implied above, personality is a complex idea. There are many psychological features on which people vary, and scientists differ on those they consider central to understanding personality and the primary influences on its development (Carducci 2009). A good theory can help psychologists organise these many personality characteristics and influences into a meaningful picture or map that can guide them when helping people. To help understand personality, sport psychologists have drawn on theories from the parent discipline, psychology, where theorists have proposed different approaches to the topic. In the following sections the major ones are described: the psychodynamic, biological, humanistic, trait and social-cognitive approaches.

PSYCHODYNAMIC

According to psychodynamic approaches, behaviour is influenced by the interactions among people's conscious and unconscious mental processes, such as needs and motivations. Sigmund Freud was one of the earliest proponents of a psychodynamic approach and suggested that personality consisted of the id, ego and superego (Freud 1916/1973). The id is the source of mental energy and has two drives: Eros, the drive for life, love and sex, and Thantos, the drive for death and aggression. The id seeks to satisfy the urge for pleasure. The superego represents internalised moral standards learned from parents and others in society. The ego represents rational thought and tries to delay the id's attempts to satisfy people's urges until suitable occasions. The ego mediates the id's and superego's interactions. The conflicts among the id, superego and ego results in anxiety, and if unable to deal with these emotions consciously, people engage in defence mechanisms that help them to deny, change, or modify reality. There are many possible defence mechanisms such as pushing unwanted thoughts into the unconscious or transforming negative emotions into positive actions. Mentally healthy people typically make use of defence mechanisms in adaptive ways. Pathological behaviour emerges when people's defence mechanisms are unable to process anxiety adequately leading to maladaptive actions.

Psychodynamic approaches have only sporadically appeared in sport psychology literature, partly because they are difficult to test and are believed to give insufficient emphasis to situational influences on behaviour. There is recognition among some sport psychologists, however, that psychodynamic ideas can help explain athletes' personalities and behaviour in sport. Psychodynamic approaches, for example, highlight that athletes are not always aware of why they behave in certain ways and may be influenced by unconscious needs and motivations. Also, some of the ways athletes approach sport echo psychodynamic defence mechanisms, such as sublimation (e.g. when a losing coach indicates the team needs to turn a negative into a positive).

BIOLOGICAL

Biological approaches focus on the extent to which genes and physiological factors may account for variations in personality and behaviour among groups of people. The Ancient Greeks proposed that personality styles could be linked to bodily fluids (e.g. people with too much blood had a sanguine personality, and they are excitable and hopeful). More contemporary approaches focus on examining how biological, psychological and environmental factors interact to determine behaviour and personality.

Although most sport psychologists recognise that behaviour may result from the interactions among biological, psychological and environmental factors, most theories in the field are not detailed enough to explain what specific physiological factors interact with others to predict particular behaviours and personality characteristics. As a result, although intuitively appealing, biological approaches have not influenced the field as much as others.

HUMANISTIC

Humanists emphasise personal worth and dignity, adopting a positive approach to understanding people. People are considered good, active and creative agents, who are motivated towards personal growth and self-fulfilment. Humanist thinkers state that to understand behaviour and personality, people's subjective interpretations of reality need to be known, because their perceptions, rather than reality itself, influences their actions.

Another key tenant is that people are motivated towards self-actualisation or to become the person the individual wants or needs to be. Self-actualisation is summed up in Maslow's (1943, one of the leaders in the field) eloquent quote: 'A musician must make music, an artist must paint, a poet must write, if he [or she] is to be ultimately happy' (p. 382). Humanist sport psychologists might assume athletes must play sport if they are to be happy and fulfilled.

Humanistic ideas have influenced many sport psychologists, as evidenced by the frequency that practitioners adopt such views in their work with athletes (Walker 2010). These practitioners often draw on Carl Rogers' person-centred approach to psychotherapy when helping clients. This eminent psychologist developed person-centred therapy or counselling (also known as client-centred counselling) in the 1940s and 1950s (Rogers 1957). The psychologist's aim in person-centred therapy is to provide clients with opportunities to develop self-awareness of how their perceptions, attitudes, thoughts, feelings, actions, reactions and behaviour are being affected negatively and are influencing their health and happiness. With this self-knowledge, clients are able to make efforts to find their true positive potential and attain meaning and fulfilment. In person-centred therapy, psychologists create a comfortable, non-judgemental relationship by being congruent (or genuine), demonstrating empathy and offering unconditional positive regard towards clients. By adopting a non-directive approach, psychologists allow clients to find their own solutions to their problems. For example, instead of telling an archer how to control anxiety, a sport psychologist might provide a relationship and psychological space in which the athlete can explore why he is getting anxious and how he can resolve the issue.[1]

TRAIT

Traits are enduring and consistent ways of behaving, and are typically described as existing on a continuum. For example, trait anxiety refers to a person's tendency to perceive non-dangerous events as threatening and respond with high levels of anxiety. Each person is believed to have some level of the trait or likelihood to display anxiety symptoms in response to non-dangerous events. Some people have a low likelihood and others have a higher tendency to experience anxiety. Whereas traits are enduring and consistent ways of behaving, states are feelings, thoughts and behaviours that people are experiencing 'right now' or at the present moment and can change quickly as situations and people change.

A contemporary trait theory that has become popular and has gained acceptance among many psychologists is the five-factor model in which similar traits are grouped under five dimensions, as illustrated in Table 1.1. Some of the dimensions, such as neuroticism and conscientiousness, have sometimes been related with sport performance (Piedmont *et al.* 1999). Much research within the trait perspective has been descriptive and cross-sectional. Referring back to Box I.1 in the Introduction, descriptive research cannot determine if these traits influence performance or if performance influences these traits (an experiment is needed to find out if traits influence

Table 1.1: The dimensions of the five-factor model

Dimension	Description
Extraversion	Includes energy, talkativeness, positive emotions, assertiveness, sociability and a tendency to seek the company of others
Agreeableness	A tendency to be compassionate and cooperative instead of suspicious or antagonistic towards others
Conscientiousness	A tendency towards self-discipline, acting dutifully and aiming for achievement
Neuroticism	A tendency to experience unpleasant emotions easily (anger, anxiety, depression, vulnerability). Refers to emotional stability and impulse control
Openness to experience	Appreciation for art, emotion, adventure, unusual ideas, creativity and a variety of experiences. Openness reflects intellectual curiosity, creativity and preference for novelty and variety

performance). Perhaps there is another variable that influences both performance and the trait. For example, maybe a good coach helps athletes develop their performance levels and conscientiousness. An over-reliance on descriptive research is one reason why a number of sport psychologists have been critical of trait theories. Another reason is that they believe trait approaches often do not acknowledge sufficiently the influence the situation has on behaviour.

SOCIAL-COGNITIVE

Social-cognitive theorists emphasise cognitive processes in understanding people's characteristics and behaviours. Example cognitive processes include the way people organise information, their decision-making strategies and their evaluation of the possible consequences of their actions. For example, athletes' likelihood of taking illegal performance-enhancing substances may be influenced by:

- their evaluation of their skill level relative to other performers (information processing);
- their beliefs about how much improvement they will gain from consuming drugs (consequence evaluation);
- the amount of time and effort they spend preparing for competition (degree of self-regulation).

In this example, athletes may be predicted to use illegal substances if they think others have greater skill levels, they will benefit a lot from ingesting them, and they cannot conceive of other ways to improve performance. Although social-cognitive theorists acknowledge that the environment influences behaviour, they argue it does so through the filters provided by people's worldviews. As an example, the degree to which a coach successfully enhances desirable training behaviours in a youth team through increased praise will be influenced by the athletes' perceptions of the positive feedback. Some athletes may relish the positive feedback and the change in their training behaviours is likely to be larger than for those who are less moved by the coach's praise. The same environmental factor (coach praise) yields different effects depending on the players' interpretations.

The social-cognitive approach has underpinned much research and practice in sport psychology. For example, one objective of many interventions conducted by sport psychologists is to modify athlete's cognitive processes, such as helping them develop their imagery skills (visualisation) or engage in planning and self-regulation (goal-setting; see Chapter 7). Practitioners assume that helping athletes develop their cognitive skills and processes will allow them to cope effectively when placed in the competitive environment.

WHICH IS BEST?

It may seem obvious to ask which approach is correct, but it is likely that each framework has strengths and limitations. Sport psychologists do not have to use one approach exclusively, and a better question to ask is which one is most helpful for understanding and guiding practice with the specific athlete the practitioner is working with at a particular time. The answer might vary depending on the athlete and the situation. One way a personality theory can help practitioners is by guiding the selection of a suitable measurement tool to assess relevant personality characteristics. I now turn to common personality measurement techniques.

TYPICAL PERSONALITY ASSESSMENT METHODS

Measuring personality characteristics helps sport psychologists understand athletes and predict how they might react in specific situations (e.g. knowing that Buffy, from the Introduction, typically doubts herself during tight games, allows predictions about how she might react in important upcoming events). Informed sport psychologists can tailor interventions to suit athletes' temperaments and behavioural tendencies. Personality measures may also help sport psychologists collect information in ways that allow them to communicate knowledge about athletes' characteristics to clients and others. Common methods sport psychologists use to measure personality characteristics include standardised questionnaires, projective tests, behavioural observations and psychophysiological measurements.

STANDARDISED INVENTORIES

Standardised inventories contain questions presented to athletes, and to which they respond, in the same way, allowing differences among athletes to emerge. For example, athletes with higher levels of self-belief are expected to respond to good-quality self-confidence questionnaires differently to those individuals with lower levels. There are a large number of questionnaires available for sport psychologists to use, and professionals vary in their beliefs that these measurement tools provide useful information.

Many questionnaires sport psychologists use are not focused on sport, but assess personality dimensions more generally. One example, the NEO Personality Inventory – Revised (NEO-PI-R), assesses the characteristics associated with the five-factor model discussed earlier in relation to the trait approach to understanding personality (Costa and McCrae 1992). Marchant (2010), a leading Australian sport psychologist, has found the NEO-PI-R helpful for providing him with an efficient way to learn about the athletes he helps, to identify areas he can explore and follow up with clients, and examining connections between personality dimensions and behaviour over time. There are also many questionnaires focused on characteristics believed to be associated with athlete behaviour and performance. For example, Martens and colleagues' (1990) Competitive State Anxiety Inventory-2 assesses athletes' state levels of cognitive anxiety, somatic anxiety and self-confidence, and scores have been correlated with performance.

Before selecting a questionnaire to use with a client, sport psychologists need to ensure the test is of high quality; otherwise the information may not help, or may even hinder, athletes' achievement of their goals. For example, a consultant who wants to measure an athlete's desire to build muscle can consider using Yelland and Tiggemann's (2003) Drive for Muscularity Scale (Figure 1.1). The practitioner would read the scientific literature to see if the scale is valid and reliable. A valid scale measures what it purports to measure: does Yelland and Tiggemann's scale actually assess the drive for muscularity? A reliable scale yields the same result or score when used in a similar way over time or tester. In the case of Yelland and Tiggemann's questionnaire, the practitioner would read that there is some evidence it is a valid and reliable scale. The practitioner may then be confident that the questionnaire will be helpful.

Even when using standardised questionnaires of high quality, there are benefits and trade-offs to their use. These questionnaires are easy to use, because the administration and scoring is standardised

For each item, decide if the item is true about you:

A	U	O	S	R	N
Always	Usually	Often	Sometimes	Rarely	Never

1	If I lose any muscle tone, I worry that I'll continue to become less muscular	A U O S R N
2	I am terrified of looking like I am not strong	A U O S R N
3	I am preoccupied with the desire to be more muscular	A U O S R N
4	I think about building up my muscles	A U O S R N
5	I feel guilty if I don't work out	A U O S R N
6	I exaggerate or magnify the importance of muscles	A U O S R N
7	I lift weights to become more muscular	A U O S R N

Figure 1.1: Yelland and Tiggemann's (2003) Drive for Muscularity Scale.

and each test-taker is treated in the same way. Standardisation also reduces administrator subjective bias, helping to enhance reliability. Standardisation may also help to assess change over time, allowing practitioners and athletes to evaluate if sport psychology interventions have been helpful. Nevertheless, standardised questionnaires rely on athletes being honest, as well as being aware of their own thoughts, feelings and behaviours. If athletes, for example, think the coach might use the results to select the starting line-up, then they may be tempted to give answers they think will be valued.

Ethically, practitioners who are members of professional bodies, such as the British Psychological Society[2] or the American Psychological Association[3] are mandated to only use tests for which they are competent. If not trained in the use of standardised questionnaires, a number of issues may arise, reducing or eliminating the value of their use. For example, poorly trained practitioners may select unsuitable or poor-quality tests, administer and score tests incorrectly, misinterpret results, or report results without considering ethical principles or how clients might react (such as sharing results with coaches and breaking athlete–practitioner confidentiality). When used competently and ethically, standardised questionnaires can help practitioners find out more about their clients, although they are not error-free and are best used as part of a range of assessment methods.

PROJECTIVE TESTS

When completing projective tests, individuals respond to ambiguous stimuli and their answers reveal aspects about their personalities, including those parts of which they are aware and unaware (or may be reluctant to express openly). Murray's (1943) Thematic Apperception Test, for example, consists of a series of cards containing black-and-white illustrations of a person or people in ambiguous situations (a blank card is also included). In constructing a story or explanation of what is happening, individuals reveal their personalities and inner worlds, including their conscious and unconscious hopes, dreams, desires, anxieties, fears and conflicts.

Although sport psychologists have not commonly used projective tests, in recent years there has been growing appreciation for the contributions they make to helping practitioners initiate dialogue with, and learn about, their clients. The Gibbs Athlete Apperception Technique (AAT) is an example of a sport-specific projective test (Gibbs 2006, 2010). Currently the AAT consists of three sets of sport images. Figure 1.2 contains an example image. There is an adult set of 10 images designed to evoke themes such as relationships with other athletes and coaches, anxiety and arousal issues, concentration, leadership, team cohesion, preparation and routines, flow and optimal performance, confidence, motivation, attributional styles and self-talk. A supplementary set consists of five images that evoke themes such as apprehension over body contact, vulnerability, arousal-aggression, faith, boasting or gloating, and conflict. The child set evokes themes including sport development and barriers. Like many projective tests, Gibbs argued that his test is designed to be used as part of a battery of assessment techniques rather than as a standalone instrument.

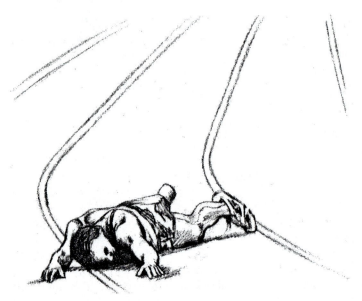

Figure 1.2: An example picture from the Athlete Apperception Test (used with permission).

Projective tests allow athletes freedom to bring up material relevant to their issues (either consciously or unconsciously) and do not force them to focus on specific information as may occur with standardised questionnaires. Projective tests may lead to a holistic understanding of the individual. It may also be difficult for athletes to distort their responses based on what they believe projective tests are attempting to measure. Critics highlight the lack of evidence for projective tests' validity and reliability, especially compared with many standardised questionnaires. Such attacks may be unfair, however, because projective tests are typically not designed to be scored or used in similar ways to standardised inventories. Whereas standardised questionnaires aim to yield information about specific targeted characteristics, such as anxiety, projective tests allow for a global understanding of people and their relevant psychological characteristics. Nevertheless, psychologists using projective tests need to be reflective about how they score or interpret clients' responses, because they may reveal more about themselves than their clients.

BEHAVIOURAL OBSERVATIONS

When using questionnaires or projective tests, athlete's perceptions, even about themselves, may be biased and limited by the boundaries of their self-understanding. Behavioural observations allow sport psychologists to access another stream of data to help them understand their clients, and involve the systematic recording and evaluation of behaviour. Sport psychologists get to see athletes perform, behave and interact with others (coaches, teammates, supporters) when competing, training and away from the sporting context. If practitioners observe athletes over time, then they may be in a position to evaluate the effectiveness of any interventions they have implemented (Watson and Shannon 2010).

As one example, Smith and colleagues' (1977) Coaching Behaviour Assessment System (CBAS) guides the observation of coaching behaviour during competition and training. Individuals using the CBAS record their observations of coaches' behaviours into one of 12 categories listed in Table 1.2. These behaviours are also classified as either reactive or spontaneous actions. Reactive

Table 1.2: Reactive and spontaneous behaviours associated with the coaching behaviour assessment system (Smith *et al.*, 1977)

Behaviour	Explanation
Reactive behaviours	
Reinforcement	A reward for a desired action
Non-reinforcement	Absence of a response to a desired action
Mistake-contingent encouragement	Encouragement given after a mistake
Mistake-contingent technical instruction	Instruction given after a mistake
Punishment	Negative reaction following undesired action
Punitive technical instruction	Punitive instruction given after a mistake
Ignoring mistakes	Absence of a response to a mistake
Keeping control	Reaction designed to maintain control
Spontaneous behaviours	
General technical instruction	Spontaneous instruction
General encouragement	Spontaneous encouragement
Organisation	Administrative behaviour
General communication	Non-sport-related communication

behaviours immediately follow athletes' desired or undesired actions, and include reinforcement, non-reinforcement, mistake-contingent encouragement, mistake-contingent technical instruction, punishment, punitive technical instruction, ignoring mistakes and keeping control. Spontaneous behaviours include general technical instruction, general encouragement, organisation and general communication. Researchers have revealed that the CBAS identifies different patterns of behaviour among coaches of various skill levels.

Observations allow professionals to view athlete behaviour in the natural setting and notice any environmental or social influences on behaviour. Observing athletes' performances and reactions may also provide information for practitioners to discuss with clients at future meetings. Behaviour observation systems are typically flexible and can easily be adapted to suit different situations. One weakness is that the amount of data that can be collected is large, and professionals need to make judgements about what information to collect: observation is open to being influenced by sport psychologists' subjective biases. Observations may be ambiguous and difficult to interpret because it is sometimes unclear how behaviour and situational factors are related to the personality dimensions of interest. For example, changes in talking (either more or less), going to the toilet often or feeling nauseous are possible signs of anxiety, but it may be difficult to assume that athletes exhibiting these behaviours are anxious (they may instead be tired, sick or excited). Although observations take place in the field (or on the court, by the track, etc.), the knowledge that sport psychologists are watching may lead to changes in athletes' behaviours and actions, either consciously or subconsciously.

PSYCHOPHYSIOLOGICAL MEASUREMENT

Although used much less often than standardised questionnaires, collecting physiological data about bodily functions may yield insights into athletes' characteristics. As a common example, sport psychologists might use physiological data such as heart rate, sweat response, skin temperature and muscle tension to examine athlete anxiety. Similarly, they may track eye movement to gain insights into attention and concentration. They might also be interested in whether hormones, such as testosterone, may be related to performance or other variables, such as aggression. Physiological measures may form the basis of interventions that help athletes, a situation labelled biofeedback. In biofeedback, athletes learn to monitor and control a bodily function. For example, New Zealand scientists showed that athletes given information about their heart rate, ventilation and oxygen consumption, and who were taught a relaxation technique, were able to improve their running economy (Caird *et al.* 1999).

Similar to behavioural observations, physiological measurements can be ambiguous and not easy to link to specific personality states and characteristics. A thumping heart rate, although a possible sign of anxiety, does not necessarily mean athletes are anxious. There are a great number of physiological measures that could be assessed and their suitability may change from situation to situation. Also, there is variation in the way athletes' physiological functions react to specific stimuli and these measures can change quickly, sometimes without explanation.

PERSONALITY MEASUREMENT: CONCLUSION

Given that each personality assessment method has limitations that influence the quality and breadth of information collected, many sport psychologists have argued that using more than one tool leads to a better understanding of an athlete's characteristics than when used in isolation. The assessment techniques practitioners use also often reflect the personality theories from which they operate. Projective tests, for example, are associated with the psychodynamic theory. Another reason for using a variety of assessment tools may be because there are different types of personality characteristics and they could relate to behaviour and performance in different ways. The relationship personality characteristics have with performance has occupied a large amount of sport psychologists' time over the years and is the focus of the next section.

WHAT IS THE RELATIONSHIP BETWEEN PERSONALITY AND PERFORMANCE?

As discussed above, sport psychologists have wondered if personality characteristics influence sports performance and have conducted numerous studies to this end. Such a broad question, however, is not easy to answer, because there are various types of sports (e.g. contact, non-contact, team, individual) for which different characteristics could lead to success. Also, there are numerous personality characteristics along which athletes might vary. When reviewing the large number of studies from the 1960s and 1970s, Morgan (1980) argued that one way to understand the personality and sports performance relationship was to consider the role of traits, states and cognitive strategies. In the following sections we will examine the major trends for each of these groupings.

PERSONALITY TRAITS

In the late seventies and early eighties, Morgan suggested there were two camps in the sport psychology community. In one camp lived the professionals who considered that personality traits could predict sports performance. In the second camp were those people who believed traits did not predict performance. Today, there are still professionals living in each camp, although sceptics outnumber believers. Although professionals' interpretations may vary, their conclusions reflect different emphases on a similar theme, rather than being mutually incompatible viewpoints. Most professionals acknowledge that limitations within the research have contributed to the lack of definitive robust answers. For example, investigators have used different criteria to distinguish between athletes and non-athletes: a person considered an athlete in one study may be classified as a non-athlete in another investigation. As another example, research has not been able to establish if certain personality traits lead to sporting success or if sporting success leads specific personality traits being developed. When the waters are muddied, it is difficult to view the fish. Given that most professionals broadly agree that research has not yielded definitive answers, it is understandable that they generally counsel against the use of trait measures for purposes such as player selection, especially without reference to other information such as recent performance or physical conditioning data.

PERSONALITY STATES

Researchers have examined the relationship between mood and performance. The Profile of Mood States (POMS) questionnaire has been used most often to measure mood in the sporting context. The POMS measures anger, depression, confusion, fatigue, tension and vigour. Based on research conducted throughout the seventies, Morgan (1980) proposed that successful athletes had an 'iceberg profile' relative to the general population, so named because of the shape of the graph as illustrated in Figure 1.3. When scores from the POMS are transformed so that the averages from the general population equal 50, then successful athletes score lower on anger, confusion, depression, fatigue and tension, but higher on vigour. Morgan also called his iceberg profile the Mental Health Model.

The iceberg profile stimulated much research, and even today sport psychologists continue to use the POMS frequently. Based on meta-analytic research (Beedie *et al.*, 2000), researchers found that moods measured by the POMS were not related to ability levels. Athletes of different levels reported similar mood profiles. When measured before a competitive event, however, mood states were related with performance. Specifically, better performance was associated with vigour, and poorer performance was related to confusion, fatigue and depression. Anger and tension were sometimes

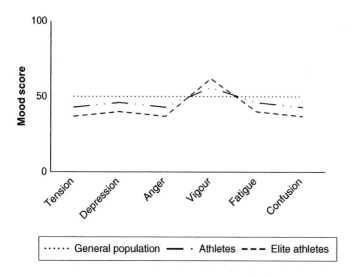

Figure 1.3: Morgan's Mental Health Model or iceberg profile.

related with better, and sometimes with worse, performance. The relationships were a little stronger for open skill sports (e.g. soccer), individual, or short-duration sports, than for closed skill sports (e.g. golf), team, and longer-duration sports. Also, the relationship was stronger when performance was measured subjectively (e.g. athlete self-rating) rather than objectively. In all cases, however, the relationships were not strong. As another limitation, just because there is a relationship does not imply that moods cause performance, only that the two variables are related. Maybe performance influences mood and not the other way around (i.e. good performances may lift athletes' moods). Alternatively, maybe another factor, such as supportive teammates leads to both better mood and performance.

COGNITIVE (AND BEHAVIOURAL) STRATEGIES

Cognitive and behavioural strategies include the deliberate thoughts and actions athletes employ to ensure their attention, cognitions, feelings and behaviours contribute to performance and goal achievement. These cognitive and behavioural strategies represent the most external dimensions of personality and may be the easiest characteristics to learn or modify. They will be easier to modify than traits (which are enduring and persistent behaviours) and unconscious impulses. There is some agreement among sport psychologists that cognitive and behavioural strategies are associated with enhanced sports performance (Krane and Williams 2010). The following strategies are typically identified by sport psychologists as being associated with enhanced performance:

- goal-setting
- imagery
- self-talk
- arousal and anxiety management
- attention control
- competition plans
- refocusing plans
- competition simulation during training.

One reason athletes use cognitive and behavioural strategies is to help them attain the Ideal Performance State, or the right profile of mental and physical states that allow them to perform their best. Athletes also use these strategies for other reasons as well, such as to deal with injury rehabilitation or cope with stress. Some sport psychologists have developed psychological skills training programmes or packages designed to teach athletes to use these strategies for performance enhancement. There are also a large number of books and multimedia materials available containing these pre-packaged programmes. The degree that these materials are helpful may be influenced by the extent to which athletes are able to apply, adapt and tailor the strategies to their specific circumstances and personal tendencies. The process of tailoring the strategies might be more easily accomplished with the help of a sport psychology professional than without. More details about these psychological skills training programmes are included in Chapter 7.

CONCLUSION

Many people believe that sporting success is influenced by a range of physical, social and psychological characteristics. It may be intuitive that jockeys benefit from having a different body type to Sumo wrestlers and that help from coaches and supporters contributes to sporting success. Asking groups of individuals to identify the personality characteristics of elite athletes generally leads to similar clusters of answers including being tough-minded, focused, disciplined, imperious to pain and criticism, confident, coachable and dedicated. To date, however, the research examining the personality–performance relationship has not yielded comparable straightforward answers. Nevertheless, the science does imply that those characteristics that help athletes adapt their behaviour to the needs of the situations in which they perform have the best relationship with performance (i.e. cognitive and behavioural strategies). One role of sport psychology is to provide professionals with mechanisms to identify and assess relevant personality characteristics. A second role is to provide interventions that help athletes develop those relevant characteristics. Some of these interventions will be detailed in Chapters 7 and 8. In Chapters 2–6, I will explore other athlete and environment dimensions relevant to sports performance.

NOTES

1 The following YouTube video illustrates the technique: http://www.youtube. com/watch?v=DjTpEL8acfo.

2 http://www.bps.org.uk.

3 http://www.apa.org.

REFERENCES

Beedie, C. J., Terry, P. C. and Lane, A. M. (2000). The profile of mood states and athletic performance: two meta-analyses. *Journal of Applied Sport Psychology, 12*, 49–68.

Caird, S. J., McKenzie, A. D. and Sleivert, G. G. (1999). Biofeedback and relaxation techniques improves running economy in sub-elite long distance runners. *Medicine and Science in Sports and Exercise, 31*, 717–722.

Carducci, B. J. (2009). *The psychology of personality: Viewpoints, research, and applications* (2nd ed.). Chichester: Wiley-Blackwell.

Costa, P. T., Jr. and McCrae, R. R. (1992). Normal personality assessment in clinical practice: The NEO personality inventory. *Psychological Assessment, 4*, 5–13.

Fisher, A. C. (1984). New directions in sport personality research. In J. M. Silva, III. and R. S. Weinberg (Eds), *Psychological foundations of sport* (pp. 70–80). Champaign, IL: Human Kinetics.

Freud, S. (1916/1973). Introductory lectures on psychoanalysis (J. Strachey, Trans.). In J. Strachey and A. Richards (Eds), *The Penguin Freud library* (Vol. I, pp. 37–557). London: Penguin.

Gibbs, P. M. (2006). *Development of the Athlete Apperception Test (ATT)*. Victoria University, Melbourne, Australia.

Gibbs, P. M. (2010). Projective techniques. In S. J. Hanrahan and M. B. Andersen (Eds), *Routledge handbook of applied sport psychology* (pp. 101–110). London: Routledge.

Krane, V. and Williams, J. M. (2010). Psychological characteristics of peak performance. In J. M. Williams (Ed.), *Applied sport psychology: Personal growth to peak performance* (6th ed., pp. 169–188). Boston: McGraw Hill.

Marchant, D. B. (2010). Objective/self-report measures. In S. J. Hanrahan and M. B. Andersen (Eds), *Routledge handbook of applied sport psychology* (pp. 111–119). London: Routledge.

Martens, R., Vealey, R. S. and Burton, D. (1990). *Competitive anxiety in sport*. Champaign, IL: Human Kinetics.

Maslow, A. H. (1943). A theory of human motivation. *Psychological Review, 50*, 370–396.

Morgan, W. P. (1980). The trait psychology controversy. *Research Quarterly for Exercise and Sport, 51*, 50–76.

Murray, H. A. (1943). *Thematic apperception test manual*. Cambridge, MA: Harvard University Press.

Piedmont, R. L., Hill, D. C. and Blanco, S. (1999). Predicting athletic performance using the five factor model of personality. *Personality and Individual Differences, 27*, 769–777.

Rogers, C. R. (1957). The necessary and sufficient conditions of therapeutic personality change. *Journal of Consulting Psychology, 21*, 95–103.

Smith, R. E., Smoll, F. L. and Hunt, E. (1977). A system for the behavioral assessment of athletic coaches. *Research Quarterly for Exercise and Sport, 48*, 401–407.

Walker, B. (2010). The humanistic/person-centered theoretical approach. In S. J. Hanrahan and M. B. Andersen (Eds), *Routledge handbook of applied sport psychology* (pp. 123–130). London: Routledge.

Watson, J. C., II. and Shannon, V. (2010). Individual and group observations: Purposes and processes. In S. J. Hanrahan and M. B. Andersen (Eds), *Routledge handbook of applied sport psychology* (pp. 90–100). London: Routledge.

Yelland, C. and Tiggemann, M. (2003). Muscularity and the gay ideal: Body dissatisfaction and disordered eating in homosexual men. *Eating Behaviors, 4*, 107-116.

2

MOTIVATION

CHAPTER LEARNING OBJECTIVES

1 Define motivation and its various subtypes (e.g. participation, achievement, self-determination).
2 Detail some major motivation theories (e.g. Atkinson's achievement motivation theory, achievement goal theory, self-determination, attribution theory).
3 Identify common themes among the various major theories.
4 Describe ways professionals can use the major theories to help people.

Coach Buttermaker had just assumed the coaching role of the Bears, an under-12-year-old softball team that had sat at the bottom of the local school league since its establishment in 1976. Coach Buttermaker, who represented his country at softball when he played, volunteered to coach because no one else was prepared to take the job and the school threatened to discontinue the team. The squad was made up of a motley group of boys and girls who joined for various reasons including liking the sport, parental pressure and wanting to spend time with friends. Coach Buttermaker wondered why the players did not seem focused on wanting to win.

During the first month of twice-a-week training, only between half and three-quarters of the players turned up on any given night. Buttermaker realised that his biggest challenge was to organise the group into a playing squad and to motivate the players to commit to the team. In his attempt to assess how competitive the team might be in the upcoming season, Buttermaker organised a warm-up game against a local school, who beat them 26–0.

Coach Buttermaker and others observing the Bears might be tempted to suggest that the players lack motivation, a concept frequently used to explain sporting success and failure. Listen to post-event interviews and you will hear athletes attributing success to their passion, drive or desire to succeed. When they fail, on talkback radio and the internet, spectators and fans frequently accuse athletes of lacking willpower, commitment or the desire to achieve. There is a pervasive belief among people involved in sport that motivation represents an internal personality characteristic that results in athletes striving to achieve success, sometimes against the odds. Such shared beliefs also underpin many sporting movies, novels and TV programmes such as *Rocky* or *Rudy*. Given the role athletes, coaches and spectators ascribe to motivation, it is understandable that sport psychologists have devoted tremendous energy to defining, measuring, examining and enhancing motivation.

Motivation, however, has proved to be much more complicated to study than might be apparent at first based on the seemingly intuitive notion that it is an internal drive to succeed. For a start, sport psychologists cannot measure motivation directly. It cannot be observed, but has to be inferred from athletes' actions, self-reports and behaviours. Also, athletes may not want to describe, or be conscious of, their motives, further making motivation an elusive concept. An American football player, for example, may not readily disclose that he enjoys hurting opponents because it is not usually a socially acceptable reason to play. Furthermore, athletes' behaviours are influenced by the environment as well as their psychological states. Any sophisticated understanding needs to consider how motivation interacts with environmental factors to appreciate its role in producing behaviour. Perhaps as a result of these difficulties, sport psychologists have developed and used a wide range of theories to describe motivation, and each approach, to some degree, captures aspects of the concept's complexity. In this chapter, I define motivation, present some of the classic or common theories and detail implications based on these frameworks.

WHAT IS MOTIVATION?

A classic definition is that motivation is a force that impels action (Sage, 1977). As an example, hunger is a force that impels people to eat. Thirst impels individuals to drink. Desire impels people to mate. Similarly in sport, motivation is often viewed as a force that drives athletes to train and compete. As a force, motivation influences the intention and effort of athletes' behaviours. Intention, or direction, refers to whether athletes choose to participate or not, and intensity refers to the amount of energy they expend in striving towards their aims. Athletes may decide that their goal (direction) is to win an Olympic medal and they may invest much time and energy (intensity) over many years to realise their dream. Alternatively, a person may choose to join a social team so they can make some new friends (direction), but coast through training (intensity) because they are more interested in socialising than in maximising their performance.

PARTICIPATION MOTIVATION

With respect to direction, sport psychologists have sought to find out why people decide to play a sport and why, once they have started, they may decide to stop. Understanding the reasons people begin or maintain involvement in a sport may help psychologists, coaches and administrators entice people to participate. Across the Western world the vast majority of people fail to attain the minimum amounts of physical activity needed to reap health benefits. Governments are interested in encouraging people to participate in physical activities, such as organised sport, to help improve health and reduce national healthcare costs. To this end, sport psychologists have researched participation motivation a great deal.

The major findings indicate that people's motives for playing and withdrawing from sport are diverse and they often have multiple reasons. Broad categories of participation motives include competence, affiliation, fitness and fun. Regarding competence, people like to participate in sport to learn and improve their skills. People can interpret their competence in relation to themselves or in comparison with others. When others-referenced, people participate in sport for competitive reasons and to gain a sense of competence from showing that they are better at the activity than others. When self-referenced, people gain a sense of competence when they believe that their skill levels are improving or they are proficient at the activity. A key finding from the participation motivation literature is that people do not always play sport for competitive reasons and the desire to win. For some people, the competitive aspect of sport is not the primary or even secondary reason they participate. For others, however, the chance to compete and the desire to win is a major reason for participating, particularly at the elite and professional level where people's livelihoods are influenced to a great extent by their ability to defeat opponents.

Regarding affiliation, fitness and fun, people often play sport for a great variety of reasons, including to: make friends; be part of a team; interact with others; improve their health; enhance appearance; be active; gain enjoyment; relieve stress; and experience sensations associated with the activity. The previous list is not exhaustive and there are many other reasons.

As well as knowing why people play sport, finding out why individuals discontinue or withdraw is also helpful to coaches and administrators. Similar to participation motives, reasons for not playing sport are varied and plentiful. Some of the common reasons include: a lack of enjoyment or fun; relationship difficulties with the coach or other players; injuries; lack of time; not getting enough (or any) playing time; an overemphasis on winning; and a desire to be involved in other activities. Some of these reasons are controllable, such as avoiding relationship difficulties by teaching coaches how to manage players or ensuring that each athlete gets a chance to play (where feasible). Other reasons for dropping out may be beyond coaches' and administrators' control, such as trying new activities or lack of time.

To encourage people to play sport, the research focused on participation motivation supports the value of tailoring marketing and promotion attempts towards the desires or reasons individuals have for being involved. Part of tailoring such marketing strategies involves identifying and understanding the target group.

For example, organisers of a club touch rugby competition may decide to de-emphasise the competitive aspects of the sport and highlight the social and fitness benefits if the people in the area most likely to be attracted are interested in meeting people, in doing something active and in engaging in an activity that allows them to mentally disengage from their jobs after work.

ACHIEVEMENT MOTIVATION

Whereas participation motivation is focused on why people decide to partake in sport, achievement motivation examines why, or why not, people may be motivated to achieve success, improve performance, master tasks and be good at their sport. Considering that success in a sporting context is often assessed relative to opponents' performances, achievement motivation is often considered in relation to competitiveness. Competitiveness may be defined as the desire to reach a level of performance that is higher than others in the presence of evaluative others (Weinberg and Gould, 2011). Achievement motivation is broader and focuses on athletes' predispositions towards striving for success and how specific situations influence their desires, emotions and behaviours. In the following sections examples of major achievement motivation theories are presented.

ATKINSON'S ACHIEVEMENT THEORY

Atkinson's (1964) theory was one of the early models sport psychologists used to understand athletes' achievement motivation. One basic premise underlying the model is that people have desires to achieve success and avoid failure. Whether or not they are motivated to engage in a specific activity results from a balance among their desire to succeed, their wish to avoid failure and how likely they believe they will succeed or fail in their attempts. A hockey player, for example, with a high need to avoid failure and who believes that she is unlikely to play well in a preseason trial game may decide not to try out for a team. Atkinson's model includes several factors to help predict the likelihood of a person engaging in achievement behaviour, including personality factors, situational factors, behavioural tendencies, emotional reactions and achievement behaviour.

Regarding personality factors, athletes have a desire to achieve success and a desire to avoid failure. People may be high in one and low in the other, high in both or low in both. Their desires may also change as they move among different situations. People high in the need for success and low in the need to avoid failure will likely think about the benefits from succeeding in the task, such as the pride and satisfaction of achieving their goals. People low in the need for success and high in the need to avoid failure will likely focus on the negative consequences of failing at the task, such as the shame and negative feelings associated with failure. To illustrate, when teaching achievement motivation I have sometimes placed a fitness ball in front of the class and invited students to come and stand on the ball (with 3–4 spotters also present to prevent injury). We then discuss the reasons why people have accepted or declined the offer. Explanations such as 'seeing if I was good enough' and 'show-ing I could accept a challenge' reflect a desire to succeed. Reasons such as 'I would look silly when I fell off' and 'I would hurt myself' reflect a wish to avoid failure. We then discuss how both motives are useful. For example, it is protective to think about the possibility of being hurt in certain situations.

Situational factors include the probability that athletes can achieve success within a specific situation and the incentive value of success. The probability of success refers to the likelihood of being successful. The incentive value details to how much worth is placed on achieving the goal in the given situation. Generally, with all other things being equal, the higher the probability of success, the lower the incentive value of achievement. Mathematically, this could be defined as 'incentive value $= 1 -$ probability of success'. To provide an extreme example, the probability of me beating the world's best tennis player (or even one of moderate ability) is astro-nomically low. In contrast, I would likely have a high probability of beating my sister, who has never played tennis. The incentive value of success for me, however, is much higher in my game against the world's best than against my sister. I have much more to gain beat-ing the world's best than defeating my sister.

According to the theory, people with a high desire to attain success and a low wish to avoid failure are likely to be most moti-vated in situations where they have a 50/50 per cent chance of success (probability of 0.5). A 50/50 per cent chance provides the optimal balance between the probability and the incentive value of success. There is little pride (or a low incentive value) in beating weak opponents (a high probability of success). Also, although there is great incentive in defeating superior opponents (a high incentive value), there is a low probability of success. If given the choice, however, individuals with a low desire to achieve success, but a high wish to avoid failure, will select tasks with extreme high or low probabilities of success. Situations with minimal risk (high probability of success, but low incentive value), such as against weak opponents, is their preferred situation because they are most likely to avoid failing. Alternatively, they may seek out highly unrealistic challenges with a low probability of success, because they can rationalise losing to a much stronger athlete.

These examples show how personality and situational factors interact to influence how athletes approach competitive situations. The interaction yields two behavioural tendencies: the tendency to approach success and the tendency to avoid failure. The tendency to approach success is associated with pride and other positive emotions that result from success, the desire to favour optimally challenging situations, and good performance. The tendency to avoid failure is associated with negative emotions, the avoidance of risk and challenge, and poorer performance.

Atkinson's theory was popular throughout the 1950s and 1960s, and has influenced most contemporary approaches to achievement motivation. In recent decades, however, sport psychologists have not used it a great deal because of its complexity. Nevertheless, the model highlights how people may have multiple achievement related motives and how these desires interact with situational factors to influence thoughts, feelings and behaviours. For example, people may be high achievers in one domain (sport), but low achievers in another area (education).

ACHIEVEMENT GOAL THEORY

During the last 20 years sport psychologists have drawn on Nicholls' (1989) achievement goal theory a great deal to examine athletes' achievement motivation. According to the theory, understanding how athletes define success provides insights into their motivation. Further, there are two typical ways athletes define success, labelled the task and ego orientations. Athletes with a strong task orientation define success in relation to themselves, and they focus on self-improvement. These individuals perceive success when they are getting better at the sport. Task-oriented people are likely to be motivated to participate in sport for enjoyment and will favour activities which provide opportunities for self-improvement. Athletes with a strong ego orientation define success in relation to others and focus on demonstrating they are better performers than the other participants. For example, they will perceive success and failure when they win or lose. Participation is likely to be viewed by ego-oriented people as an opportunity to compare themselves with others and demonstrate their superior ability. They will prefer tasks that allow them to appear high in ability in comparison with others.

To help illustrate each orientation, consider the players running onto a netball court. The task-oriented players are motivated by the fact that they have been practising a specific drill designed to help them to improve their game. Although they may still value winning, they will measure their success by how well they and the team perform. The ego-oriented players will want to beat the other team, and also likely want to outshine their teammates. Although defined separately, athletes are not either task or ego oriented, but they may also be high or low in both. Many elite athletes, for example, have high levels of both task and ego orientation. Alternatively, some people may be low in both task and ego orientation, and these individuals may well withdraw from sport, unless there are other reasons for participating, such as being with friends.

Achievement goal theory makes a number of predictions regarding the types of behaviours that are associated with the two orientations (Harwood *et al.* 2008). For example, a high task orientation is predicted to be related with an adaptive achievement behavioural pattern including: sustained engagement in training; high effort in both training and competition; persistence in the face of difficulty; selecting optimally challenging tasks and opponents when given the choice; consistently performing close to one's potential; and continually working on skill improvement. When perceived competence is high, these achievement behaviours are predicted to also occur with a high ego orientation.

When the ego-oriented athlete has low perceived competence then the following maladaptive achievement behaviours are expected: reduced effort in training and competition; performance impairment due to anxiety over one's competence; selection of either overly difficult challenges (so the individual will not feel bad about losing) or overly easy tasks (where success is guaranteed); and potentially withdrawing from sport due to the belief that one is not competent. There is research to support many of these predictions. As stated above, however, athletes may have both orientations to various degrees (high task/low ego, low task/high ego, etc.). The studies that have examined the various profiles suggest that a high ego orientation is not detrimental as long as there is also a strong task orientation.

More broadly, the orientations are also related with beliefs about the causes of success, perceptions about the purposes of sport, emotions and sportsmanship attitudes. A high task orientation is correlated with the belief that hard work leads to success, perceptions that sport is an avenue to promote mastery, cooperation and social responsibility, and enjoyment and satisfaction. In contrast, a high ego orientation is associated with the belief that ability and deception leads to success, and sport's purpose is to enhance the self (e.g. popularity, wealth and social status). There is a negative relationship with enjoyment and satisfaction. Also, a high ego orientation, low task orientation and low perceived ability are related with unsporting attitudes and willingness to take any unfair advantage to ensure winning and demonstrating superior ability.

The discussion above has described goal orientations as personality dispositions. Researchers, however, have also explored whether people have situation specific goals, known as 'goal involvement'. Somebody who is primarily ego oriented, for example, may display task involvement in situations where the focus is on personal improvement. Another athlete, who is primarily task oriented, might display ego involvement during a competitive match if there is an emphasis on winning the game. Broadly in sport, athletes might tend to be task involved during training, when the focus is on skill development and competition preparation, but ego involved during competitive events when performance is being evaluated normatively. One likely influence on goal involvement is the motivational climate. Motivational climate refers to the influence the social environment has on individuals' motivation, and with regards to achievement goal theory, describes the degree that the leaders in the situation promote either task mastery or social comparison goals. A mastery climate is one where a coach or leader encourages a task involvement through supportive comments when athletes persist, improve and help others through teamwork. A competitive climate fosters ego involvement through the use of competition and comparison as a basis for athlete evaluation (Duda and Balaguer 2007).

A perceived mastery climate has been associated with positive achievement behaviours, thoughts and emotions. Examples include: (a) enjoyment and satisfaction; (b) the belief that effort leads to success; (c) subjective and objective measures of performance; (d) adaptive coping strategies; (e) reduced burnout; (f) perceptions that coaches provide positive feedback, training, instruction and support; (g) perceived competence; (h) team cohesion and relationships; (i) the view that the purposes of sport include fostering a work ethic and prosocial values; (j) an endorsement of positive moral values; and (k) less self-handicapping.

A perceived competitive climate has been correlated with a maladaptive pattern of behaviour, thoughts and emotions. Specific examples include: (a) anxiety; (b) the belief that ability determines success; (c) dropping out of sport; (d) team conflict; (e) defining success in comparison with others; (f) perceiving that coaches provide punishment rather than positive or supportive feedback; (g) less developed moral reasoning and behaviour; and (h) self-handicapping.

SELF-DETERMINATION THEORY

Many motivation theories help sport psychologists understand goal content, or the things athletes want to achieve, such as self-improvement or showing they are better than others. Self-determination theory differentiates goal content from the regulatory processes by which goals are pursued (e.g. do people feel they are in control of their choice to strive for a goal) and the degree to which these goals satisfy some underlying needs shared by all people (Ryan and Deci 2007). Self-determination theory is a broad framework that consists of a number of sub-components that attempt to explain why humans often appear to initiate and maintain engagement in activities for their own sake and frequently in the absence of external rewards. It is beyond the scope of the current chapter to present self-determination theory in full and the Further Reading provides some key suggested sources. Self-determination theory has relevance for the sporting context, because most people who play sport do so voluntarily at a sub-elite level, and may devote considerable time, money and effort without the return of the external material gains or social status accorded to elite professional performers. As such, sport provides opportunities to investigate intrinsic motivation, a key construct in self-determination theory. Intrinsic motivation refers to the desire to engage in a sport for the satisfaction inherent in the activity. For example, a person may engage in weightlifting because of the satisfaction gained from attempting and succeeding at the various competitive lifts.

Within self-determination theory, the degree to which athletes are intrinsically motivated is influenced by the ways in which their social environments facilitate or hinder the satisfaction of three psychological needs: competence, autonomy and relatedness. Competence refers to athletes' perceptions that they are able to perform the sport and achieve desired outcomes. Autonomy refers to athletes' beliefs that they are free to choose to participate, rather than being controlled by others. Relatedness refers to athletes' perceptions that they are connected and supported by others and feel included in the group. Intrinsic motivation is enhanced when social environments facilitate the satisfaction of these psychological needs. If environments thwart the satisfaction of these psychological needs then intrinsic motivation is decreased. Coaches, for example, who focus on skill improvement (enhance competence), build team cohesion (develop relatedness) and allow athletes to have a say in how the team is organised (encourage autonomy) are likely to enhance participants' intrinsic motivation. Attempts, however, to control athlete behaviour through contingent rewards (that reduce autonomy), conditional acceptance (lowering relatedness) and destructive criticism (that decreases perceived competence) are likely to reduce intrinsic motivation.

The theory also acknowledges that athletes often have multiple motives for participation, some of which are intrinsic and others that are extrinsic. Extrinsic motivation refers to the desire to participate for outcomes not inherent to the activity. Playing soccer for the possibility of obtaining a professional contract and earning money is an example of an extrinsic motive. Athletes may also experience amotivation or have a lack of desire to participate or expend effort in the sport. Such athletes are likely to withdraw from the sport. There are various types of extrinsic motivation that can be placed on a continuum reflecting the degree to which they are internalised by the athlete and reflect perceived autonomy, as illustrated in Figure 2.1. When motivated by external regulation, athletes participate for the rewards imposed by externally defined goals, such as when parents pressure children into playing tennis because of the potential financial rewards. When motivated out of introjected regulation, athletes control their own participation through reward and punishment. Runners who set a particular time in a race, for example, may promise to reward themselves by having a rest day or punish themselves by doing extra hill training. In identified regulation, athletes choose to participate in the sport because they identify with the activity's purpose and values. People may enter running races, for example, because they believe doing so will enhance their health and appearance. In integrated regulation, the reasons for participation are coherent with athletes' overall life goals, their lifestyles and their sense of identity.

The various types of motivation in Figure 2.1 represent points along a continuum. Figure 2.1 does not present a stage-like model in which people enter at one end, develop and then shed each motivation type as they move towards the other end. Instead, athletes may enter at any point in the continuum, and their movement around the various forms of regulation is influenced by the degree to which the social environment facilitates or hinders their basic psychological needs. For example, an adult may take up swimming and enter competitions because she wants to lose weight and improve her appearance, reflecting extrinsic motives. Over time, however, she might find satisfaction in the sport because it gives her a sense of competence from learning a new skill and a belief that she is making an autonomous decision to look after her health, reflecting intrinsic motives.

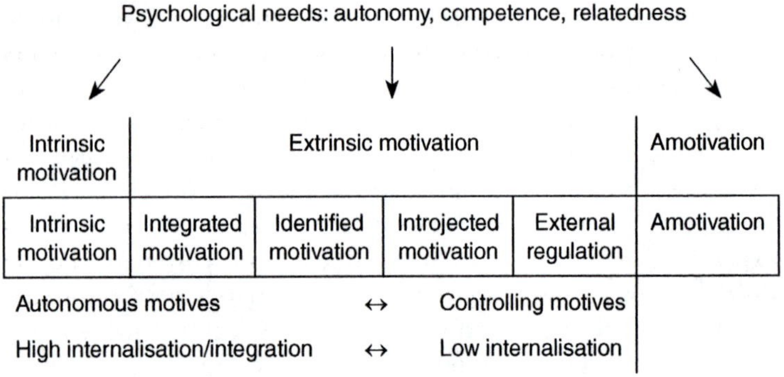

Psychological needs: autonomy, competence, relatedness

Intrinsic motivation	Extrinsic motivation				Amotivation
Intrinsic motivation	Integrated motivation	Identified motivation	Introjected motivation	External regulation	Amotivation

Autonomous motives   ↔   Controlling motives

High internalisation/integration   ↔   Low internalisation

Figure 2.1: Overview of self-determination theory. (Adapted from Ryan and Deci 2007.)

There has been much research examining the principles of self-determination theory in the sporting context and there is support that the approach provides a helpful explanation of athlete behaviour (Kingston *et al.* 2006). For example, coaching approaches that provide competence-related feedback and autonomy supportive climates are associated with self-determined regulation, persistence, increased participation, reduced dropout and enhanced performance. Coaching practices that reduce players' sense of competence, autonomy and relatedness are associated with less self-determined regulation, greater dropout, burnout and withdrawal. These results indicate that self-determination theory can help coaches consider how to structure the sporting context to enhance the satisfaction of athletes' psychological needs, promote their sense of self-determination and attain positive benefits and a rewarding high-quality sporting experience.

A common practice within sport is to give people external rewards, such as trophies, t-shirts and prizes. Within self-determination theory it is possible to explain why such practices may sometimes increase, and at times decrease, intrinsic motivation. Each external reward carries informational and controlling feedback. The informational component refers to the messages rewards convey about athletes' competence. The controlling aspects refers to the extent rewards promote an internal or external locus of causality. Regarding the informational component, athletes' intrinsic motivation will increase when rewards (or other consequences) provide positive feedback about their competence. Intrinsic motivation will be reduced when rewards or consequences are associated with negative feedback about ability. With respect to the controlling dimension, external rewards or consequences that promote an external locus of causality (or a belief that participation is influenced by sources outside of the athlete) reduce intrinsic motivation. External rewards or consequences that advocate an internal locus of causality (or the message that the athlete is instigating participation) increase intrinsic motivation.

ATTRIBUTIONS

Sport psychologists have also examined the reasons people give for the events that happen when participating in sport, under the label of attributions. Attributions refer to the perceived causes of events (Hanrahan and Biddle 2008). For example, a lacrosse player may suggest her team won because of superior skill compared with the opposition, whereas someone from the other team may suggest they lost because of poor officiating. Attributions are perceptions that will not always correspond with reality. People's attributions, however, are useful to understand because these explanations will predict behaviour, thoughts and feelings. A baseball player who frequently attributes failure to external factors despite having poor technique may not take responsibility for addressing a weakness.

Athletes give a great many reasons or attributions for their performances and other events in sport. Researchers have categorised these various reasons into a smaller number of dimensions to help understand attributions and make predictions about future behaviour. Stability, internality and controllability are common dimensions (Weiner, 1992). Stable attributions include those that will typically always be a factor in a situation, such as ability. Unstable causes include those that may or may not be present, such as good luck. Internal attributions are those that originate from within the athlete, such as effort. External causes are those stemming from outside the athlete, such as task difficulty. Controllable attributions refer to causes that athletes can change, such as effort. Uncontrollable causes are those athletes cannot alter, such as luck. The placement of attributions within specific categories is open to interpretation. For example, although ability is typically given as an example of a stable attribution, many people might believe they can change their ability with training. These individuals may class ability as an unstable attribution. It is useful to ask athletes how they interpret their own attributions.

Being able to use categories or taxonomies assists sport psychologists in understanding athletes' attribution styles. People have consistent patterns in the types of attributions they invoke when explaining events in their lives. A common pattern or bias among people is to attribute success to internal factors about themselves (e.g. ability) and failure to external causes (e.g. bad luck). Although such a bias may be viewed as self-serving, it is also possible that the bias arises from the belief that people normally intend to succeed in their endeavours. It is reasonable then to attribute success to oneself and failure to some unexpected external cause.

Being aware of attributions helps sport psychologists predict behaviour, emotions and thoughts. For example, some athletes attribute failure to stable and uncontrollable causes (e.g. 'I will always lose and I can't do anything to change the situation'). Their attributions may reflect the belief they have no control over negative events, an explanatory style labelled learned helplessness. Learned helplessness is associated with negative emotions, depression, anxiety, giving up, poor performance and avoidance. In sport, people who develop a learned helpless attitude are likely to withdraw from participating. Researchers have shown, however, that people can be taught how to change their explanatory style. Athletes, for example, can learn to believe that they can exert some level of control over negative events. Attribution retraining may also result in more positive behaviours, emotions and perceptions.

MOTIVATION THEORY LESSONS

Although sport psychologists have drawn on various motivation approaches or theories to understand athlete behaviour, there are similarities across the models. These theories might be considered like a range of fine New Zealand or Californian wines: despite having different tastes, they are still wines. Below are some common themes emerging from the approaches that help sport psychologists working with athletes.

PEOPLE HAVE VARIED AND MULTIPLE MOTIVES

The structure of sport tends to be competitive because people's performances typically get compared against others. The desire to win, however, is not the always the sole or even the main reason individuals participate in sport. At the elite and professional levels, winning is a high or the highest priority, but this is not always the case at the sub-elite levels. People vary, however, and at the sub-elite levels some athletes make competition a life or death event. Also, even at the elite level, some athletes define success in multiple ways. Sport psychologists will likely find that their attempts to assist players with motivation will benefit from listening to athletes, finding out their motives for playing sport and then building on those within the constraints of the context.

ENVIRONMENTS INFLUENCE MOTIVATION

Significant others, such as coaches, teammates, family and psychologists can influence participants' motivation. When significant others emphasise interpersonal rivalry, being better than others and results rather than performance, and when they take control over the decision-making process, motivation may change from being intrinsic and task oriented to being externally regulated and ego oriented. Conversely, when self-improvement, social support and autonomy are encouraged, then task mastery and self-determination are promoted. Research has also indicated that behaviours and thoughts, such as persistence, performance and commitment, vary with different types of motivation. Helping to promote mastery climates and intrinsic goal involvement may help athletes achieve greater success or meaning from their sports.

COMPETENCE IS NOT THE ONLY NEED SATISFIED IN SPORT

Although athletes' specific motives for participating are numerous, there are some common psychological needs that result from being a human, such as competence, autonomy and relatedness. Intuitively, competence is a psychological need present in an achievement-based activity such as sport. Research reveals, however, that finding ways to meet the other needs yields valued performance, behavioural and psychological benefits. One way in which sport psychology is an art, as opposed to a science, is to understand how best to help athletes in specific sports and situations achieve need satisfaction. For example, the ways in which relatedness needs are likely to be met in contact sports may be different from those in non-contact sports. Even the optimal methods for helping individual athletes satisfy relatedness needs may vary within specific sports. The research has not drilled down to such a fine-grained level, and practitioners need to make decisions based on their professional knowledge and experience.

TASK MASTERY IS TYPICALLY ASSOCIATED WITH POSITIVE OUTCOMES

As has been stated in several places above, a task mastery orientation has been associated with adaptive motivational behaviours and outcomes. There are various strategies that can be implemented to encourage athletes to develop a task mastery orientation. Setting up practice where possible, for example, so that drills are challenging, varied and interesting, with clear links to performance, can contribute to a task focus. Recognising and praising good performance and learning, as well as successful outcomes, is another strategy. It may also help to base evaluations of athletes' performances on their personal development instead of solely on social comparison. For example, even when athletes lose an event there is value in identifying aspects that they did well and areas where they might improve rather than just focusing on what they did poorly. Encouraging athletes to be proactive and share in the decision-making process may help them attain a sense of autonomy and ownership of their participation. Encouraging interaction among teammates may allow players to coach and learn from each other and satisfy relatedness needs.

A STRONG DESIRE TO WIN IS NOT NECESSARILY ASSOCIATED WITH NEGATIVE OUTCOMES

The maladaptive motivational and behavioural outcomes that have been associated with an ego orientation may be interpreted by some people as suggesting that a strong desire to win and demonstrate superior skill over opponents is best squashed in athletes. Before reaching such a conclusion, it is worth considering that many researchers believe that a maladaptive motivational pattern is associated with an ego orientation only when coupled with a weak task orientation or low perceived competence. Especially at the elite and professional levels, a strong desire to win is likely to be a source of motivation for attaining optimal and enhanced performance. Research has indicated that any detrimental effects of a strong ego orientation may be buffered by developing high perceived competence and a task focus. Athletes can be both ego and task oriented. Optimal performance may be achieved when they define success in both ways and have high perceived ability.

CONCLUSION

When Coach Buttermaker played softball he was competing at a high level where winning was a high priority. He may find that emphasising winning as the Bears' primary purpose demotivates some players. The players appear to have a number of reasons for being in the team. A useful place for Buttermaker to start could be to listen to the players and identify the reasons why they decided to join the team. These probably have to do with having fun, being with friends and learning new skills, as much as to do with winning. Structuring the environment to allow the satisfaction of these motives may help to attract the players to attend training more frequently. The achievement goal, self-determination and attribution theories presented in this chapter can help him identify specific ways to develop an atmosphere that is task oriented and promotes autonomy, competence and relatedness. Some example strategies were also discussed. One advantage of developing a task mastery motivational climate is that it is associated with lower levels of anxiety and stress, and these are topics addressed in the next chapter.

REFERENCES

Atkinson, J. W. (1964). *An introduction to motivation*. Oxford: Van Nostrand.

Duda, J. L. and Balaguer, I. (2007). Coach-created motivational climate. In S. Jowett and D. Lavallee (Eds), *Social psychology in sport* (pp. 117–130). Champaign, IL: Human Kinetics.

Hanrahan, S. J. and Biddle, S. J. H. (2008). Attributions and perceived control. In T. S. Horn (Ed.), *Advances in sport psychology* (3rd ed., 99–114). Champaign, IL: Human Kinetics.

Harwood, C., Spray, C. M. and Keegan, R. (2008). Achievement goal theories in sport. In T. S. Horn (Ed.), *Advances in sport psychology* (3rd ed., pp. 157–186). Champaign, IL: Human Kinetics.

Kingston, K. M., Harwood, C. G. and Spray, C. M. (2006). Contemporary approaches to motivation in sport. In S. Hanton and S. D. Mellalieu (Eds), *Literature reviews in sport psychology* (pp. 159–197). New York: Nova Science.

Nicholls, J. G. (1989). *The competitive ethos and democratic education.* Cambridge, MA: Harvard University Press.

Ryan, R. M. and Deci, E. L. (2007). Active human nature: Self-determination theory and the promotion and maintenance of sport, exercise, and health. In M. S. Hagger and N. L. D. Chatzisarantis (Eds), *Intrinsic motivation and self-determination in exercise and sport* (pp. 1–19). Champaign, IL: Human Kinetics.

Sage, G. (1977). *Introduction to motor behavior* (2nd Ed.). Boston: Addison-Wesley.

Weinberg, R. S. and Gould, D. (2011). *Foundations of sport and exercise psychology* (5th Ed.). Champaign, IL: Human Kinetics.

Weiner, B. (1992). *Human motivation: Metaphors, theories and research.* Newbury Park, CA: Sage.

AROUSAL, STRESS, ANXIETY AND PERFORMANCE

CHAPTER LEARNING OBJECTIVES

1 Define arousal, stress and anxiety.
2 Explore how professionals measure arousal, stress and anxiety.
3 Identify antecedents of anxiety in sport.
4 Overview the relationship between arousal, anxiety and performance.
5 Describe how stress influences performance.
6 Review ways professionals can help athletes cope with anxiety and stress.

Over the past year, Chuck has experienced anxiety each time he has stepped onto the floor to compete in national dance sport competitions since teaming up with his new partner, Sarah. Although he always enjoyed Latin and ballroom dancing as a child, things changed once he decided to compete. Chuck has found being evaluated by judges and spectators, and realising that his mistakes have consequences for Sarah, threatening to his sense of self. Failure means he is not good at something he likes and values, and he cannot come through for a friend when it matters. He cannot remove these thoughts from his mind prior to competition and focus on what he wants to think about, which is going over the moves in his head and reminding himself of technical features such as his body position, his hold with Sarah and his arm movements. Instead, he finds himself tense and worried to the point that his personality changes: he loses his sense of humour, becomes quiet and edgy and snaps at those around him. He seldom sleeps well the night before a competition and on two occasions has vomited from fear. He found talking to Coach Beckmann and John (a senior male dancer at the Carmichael School of Dance) unhelpful, because they simply told him to relax and focus on dancing. Chuck replied, 'ok, but how do I relax?'. He has spent a lot of time talking about his anxieties and fears with his best friend Morgan and his sister Ellie. Although talking about his worries seemed to help him relax for a short period of time, his fears would return prior to each competition. In the lead up to a competition he often recalls his first event where his mind had 'gone blank' while he was on the floor and he had not been able to remember the moves that he and Sarah had practised. Chuck was thinking of ending his partnership with Sarah and his involvement in dance sport.

Applied sport psychologists will testify that athletes commonly experience anxiety and stress. Athletes' anxieties range from mild cases of butterflies in the stomach to extreme instances, as illustrated in Chuck's story. Perhaps reflecting that these issues are widespread, sport psychologists have devoted considerable effort to understanding the causes of anxiety and stress, how they influence performance and how to help athletes manage them. In this chapter I define these terms, along with discussing how they are assessed, why they influence performance, and strategies for helping athletes.

DEFINING AROUSAL, ANXIETY AND STRESS

Athletes and coaches often use the words 'anxiety', 'stress' and 'arousal' interchangeably, and because their listeners generally know what they are trying to say it does not lead to miscommunication. Precision is needed, however, when undertaking research and implementing psychological strategies, and sport psychologists are careful to define these terms so they know what they are measuring and can communicate findings to others. As a result, to present the sport psychology knowledge clearly, it is useful to start by defining the terms.

Arousal refers to athletes' levels of activation or excitation and it exists on a continuum from low (e.g. sleep) to high (e.g. hyperactive). When sunbathing, most people have low levels of arousal. If it suddenly started raining, however, most people's arousal would increase as they jumped up to gather their towels and head inside. Increased arousal helps people prepare physical, mental and behavioural resources so they can respond to environmental demands.

Anxiety refers to the level of perceived threat that is accompanied by worry, nervousness and apprehension. A key idea in anxiety is athletes' interpretation of the danger to their wellbeing. Sometimes anxiety is a normal response to real threats, such as when individuals are confronted by an armed person. Sometimes anxiety involves an exaggerated response to an imagined threat, such as my reaction to spiders (except in Australia where they can kill you!). Anxiety is typically accompanied by high arousal, but the two are not the same. People can be highly aroused yet not anxious, such as when athletes win major competitions.

It is useful to differentiate between trait and state anxiety. In sport, competitive trait anxiety is a person's characteristic response or predisposition to perceive situations as threatening and to react with high anxiety. Competitive trait anxiety levels vary among athletes and influence state anxiety, or their right-now, moment-to-moment perceptions of threat and accompanying worries and apprehension. Athletes with high levels of competitive trait anxiety are likely to respond to sporting events with high levels of state anxiety compared with participants with low trait levels. The relationship is not perfect and state anxiety is also influenced by the situation. Athletes with high levels of trait anxiety will not respond to competitions with high state anxiousness if they do not view any threat to their wellbeing. Alternatively, athletes will low trait anxiety levels may experience high state anxiety on occasions. It would be understandable, for example, if a low-trait athlete found a high-level event nerve-wracking, such as an Olympic final.

Anxiety is also multidimensional, consisting of physical and mental components. Physical or somatic anxiety encompasses perceptions of the physiological symptoms of arousal, such as heart rate, sweat response or breathing rate. Cognitive anxiety refers to the worries, qualms, apprehensions and negative expectations athletes have about competition.

Stress is a process in which athletes perceive differences between what is being asked of them and their abilities to cope when failure has important consequences. Typically, athletes will respond to such perceived imbalances with high state anxiety. For example, a soccer player may find a game stressful if she has been unable to prepare the week before due to illness and she is aware talent scouts are present to watch her perform.

MEASURING AROUSAL, STRESS AND ANXIETY

To measure arousal, anxiety and stress, sports psychologists assess physiological, psychological or behavioural variables. Examples of physiological variables include heart rate, blood pressure and muscle tension. Psychological variables include worries, interpretations of bodily responses and decision-making. Behavioural variables include nail-biting, pacing or frequent urination. Similar to personality (see Chapter 1), sport psychologists assess these variables using physiological measures, self-report questionnaires or behavioural observations (Moran 2012).

QUESTIONNAIRES

The ease with which self-report inventories can be administered and scored is the main reason why researchers have used paper-and-pencil questionnaires most often when examining anxiety and stress in sport. The Competitive State Anxiety Inventory-2 (CSAI-2) is an example of a questionnaire that has been frequently used to measure anxiety in sport. The CSAI-2 contains 27 items that assess cognitive anxiety, somatic anxiety and self-confidence. Using a four-point Likert scale (1 = 'not at all' and 4 = 'very much so'), participants indicate the current intensity of their anxiety. An example cognitive anxiety item is 'I have self-doubts'. An example somatic anxiety item is 'I feel jittery'. One self-confidence item is 'I feel self-confident'. In more recent years, researchers have adapted the CSAI-2 to suit their needs, such as shortening it to 15 items. Also, some researchers think asking athletes whether their anxiety helps or hinders performance assists the understanding of the topic in sport. These researchers have revised the CASI-2 to allow the measurement of athletes' interpretation of the intensity of their anxiety. Specifically for each item, athletes are asked to indicate the degree to which their anxiety intensity will have a negative or positive effect on their performance.

Sport psychologists have a variety of self-report questionnaires from which they can select to assess anxiety. These questionnaires have contributed to a large body of work that details the understanding of anxiety and stress in sport. Nevertheless, the measurement of anxiety has generated much debate, partly due to the inconsistency with which the term has been used and defined and partly due to the limitations associated with the standard questionnaires. Asking people to reflect on their anxiety, for example, may alter it, perhaps making them more anxious than before they were asked. A leading researcher in the field, Uphill (2008), has recommended that people need a healthy dose of scepticism when interpreting the results from questionnaires.

PHYSIOLOGICAL MEASURES

The use of physiological measures of anxiety has been much less common compared with self-report questionnaires for various reasons. Depending on the measure, physiological assessment can be (although not always) invasive, time-consuming, inconvenient or expensive. The value of these measures may be limited, for example, if athletes have to be brought into a lab that does not replicate their place of competition. Physiological measures typically assess arousal rather than anxiety and they often do not correlate highly with each other, suggesting they are measuring different constructs. As such, they may be of limited value to researchers interested in anxiety. There is no consensus on the best physiological variable to measure for anxiety. It seems more likely that the suitable physiological variables to measure in a study may depend on the task, athlete and situation (for example, heart rate may not be a useful measure when studying weightlifting tasks). It may then be difficult to compare the research across studies. Athletes also interpret physiological sensations differently, complicating the study of their effect on performance or other outcomes. Despite these limitations, sport psychologists have advanced understanding and have helped athletes using physiological measures. One example is the use of biofeedback techniques with shooters to help them learn to fire between heartbeats to increase accuracy.

BEHAVIOURAL MEASURES

Similar to physiological measurements, sport psychologists have not undertaken behavioural observations of anxiety symptoms with the same frequency as they have used self-reported questionnaires. As with personality more generally (see Chapter 1), behaviour observations of anxiety symptoms involve professionals making judgements about what information to collect and how to score athletes' actions. As such, behavioural observations are open to being influenced by sport psychologists' subjective biases. Observations may be difficult to interpret because it may be uncertain if the behaviour represents anxiety or any other personality dimension. For example, increased levels of chatter may reflect anxiety or excitement. Also, the knowledge that sport psychologists are watching may lead to changes in athletes' behaviours and actions, either consciously or subconsciously.

WHAT ARE THE ANTECEDENTS OF ANXIETY IN SPORT?

Given the definition of anxiety, anything that leads to athletes perceiving a threat or a perceived imbalance between their abilities and the demands of the task may be an antecedent to the reaction. If the size of the opposition triggers thoughts about impending injury in a rugby league player, then anxiety may well result. If sport psychologists know of the various anxiety antecedents, then they may be able to identify ways to help athletes avoid detrimental consequences associated with these perceptions and emotions. The antecedents listed below are those most often mentioned when sport psychologists discuss factors contributing to the perception of threat and can be divided into those that relate to the environment and those that relate to the athlete.

SITUATIONAL FACTORS

- *Perceived event importance and uncertainty.* Greater perceived event uncertainty and importance are associated with higher levels of anxiety. It may not be possible to change how important an event is objectively for athletes or to reduce uncertainty about the outcome. Instead, sport psychologists may help athletes to adjust their perceptions so they place less importance on the consequences, or they are not as troubled about the degree of uncertainty. Building athletes' confidence may also reduce perceived uncertainty.

- *Type of sport.* Individual sport athletes report higher levels of anxiety than their team counterparts, perhaps because their performances are typically more obviously tied to the result and failure may be more attributable to their efforts and skill. Contact-sport participants also report higher levels of anxiety than non-contact athletes. It may be that in many contact sports there is the added perceived physical threat that might be missing from non-contact games.

- *Time to competition.* Sport psychologists have measured athletes' anxiety levels multiple times across the days leading up to a sporting event, known as the 'time to event' paradigm. Results indicate different patterns for cognitive and somatic anxiety. Cognitive anxiety appears to be stable and high in the time period approaching the event. In contrast, somatic anxiety remains low until one or two days before the event and then increases incrementally until the start of competition. The time to event paradigm does not really explain why athletes get nervous and worry, but does give some insight in to how they are feeling prior to the event.

ATHLETE FACTORS

- *Trait anxiety.* People who attain high scores on trait anxiety questionnaires are likely to interpret sport situations as threatening and respond with heightened levels of state anxiety. Given that trait anxiety questionnaires ask about how people typically respond to competition, the finding does not really explain why people become anxious (i.e. the suggestion that 'I am anxious because I normally become anxious' does not give away clues as to why anxiety has increased). The relationship between trait and state anxiety is also not perfect. Trait anxiety questionnaires rely on highly anxious people reporting that they perceive sporting situations as threatening leading to nervousness, tension, worry, etc. The connection between trait and state anxiety will reduce if people do not wish to admit or are unaware of how anxious they become before and during competition.

- *Perfectionism.* Perfectionism involves attempting to achieve flawless performances and the setting of extremely ambitious goals. Psychologists often describe perfectionism as being multifaceted with adaptive and maladaptive dimensions. Adaptive perfectionism motivates athletes to strive for success, whereas the maladaptive dimensions lead to excessive concerns about mistakes. Anxiety is associated with maladaptive perfectionism, perhaps by adversely influencing athletes' thoughts and focusing them on their mistakes and things that could go wrong.

- *Self-handicapping.* Athletes self-handicap when they reduce their effort levels and offer excuses for potential or actual poor performance to defend themselves from negative feedback. For example, a runner may pull out of a race, begin limping and highlight a recent injury if she starts to fall behind the leaders to avoid losing the race and showing that she is not as good as she hoped. It may be, however, that handicapping is an anxiety symptom rather than antecedent. Athletes may be more likely to self-handicap after they have perceived a threat rather than before. On occasion self-handicapping may serve a self-enhancement, as well as a self-protection, function. For example, the runner above would be able to say that she must be fit or resilient if she had managed to keep running and had won the race.

- *Self-perceptions and identity.* Some people invest more of themselves in their identity as athletes and their participation contributes more to their self-worth and esteem than other individuals. For these people, winning and losing may become all important, and failure can have serious negative psychological consequences. Event importance is not only an objective variable. Some athletes may perceive an event of low importance objectively to be critical. Add low perceived competence or self-confidence into the mix and these folks may be at risk for experiencing anxiety.

WHAT ARE THE RELATIONSHIPS AMONG AROUSAL, ANXIETY AND PERFORMANCE?

There are several theories explaining the relationships among arousal, anxiety and performance. Although each model contributes to understanding the relationship, they have both supportive and non-supportive research. Some of these theories are presented below to illustrate the flavour of their explanations.

DRIVE THEORY

Hull's drive theory was one of the initial models sport psychologists drew on to understand how arousal influenced performance. Hull stated that increased arousal was associated with the display of an individual's well-learned or dominant response to a stimulus. In simple tasks, or for athletes skilled in the sport, the dominant response is likely to be the correct one, and high, rather than low, arousal is hypothesised to lead to better performance. In complex tasks, or for novice athletes still learning the sport, the dominant response may not be the correct one, and increased, rather than decreased, arousal is hypothesised to lead to no change or even reduced performance. Experiments have not provided conclusive support for drive theory, leading sport psychologists to consider alternative explanations.

INVERTED-U THEORY

In 1908, Yerkes and Dodson proposed the inverted-U theory suggesting that optimal performance occurs at a moderate level of arousal. Suboptimal performance occurs when arousal is either above or below this moderate level. With gradual increases in arousal from low to moderate levels there are corresponding incremental increases in performance. Similarly, as arousal gradually increases from moderate to high levels, there are incremental decreases in performance.

Two factors that influence the effect of arousal on performance include task complexity and individual differences among athletes. In complex tasks the optimal level of arousal is lower than in simple tasks. Such differences may apply across and within sports. For example, the optimal level of arousal needed by darts throwers is likely to be lower than that for wrestlers. Similarly, within

American football, the optimal level of arousal for a defensive lineman is probably higher than for the goal kicker.

Some athletes will perform better when they are highly aroused, whereas others will do so when relaxed and calm. For example, athletes with high levels of trait anxiety will likely become anxious with increased arousal and their worries and tension may hinder performance. They will perform best at a low arousal level. In contrast, athletes with low trait anxiety levels are less likely to become anxious with increased arousal. These athletes might find low levels of arousal are associated with poor performance because they are not motivated enough to organise and focus all their physical, mental and behavioural resources on the task at hand.

Similar to the drive theory, research support for the inverted-U theory in sporting contexts has been mixed. Perhaps due to the mixed results, sport psychologists have criticised the inverted-U theory for a number of reasons. For example, arousal is multidimensional, with physical, mental and behavioural components, yet the inverted-U theory describes the construct as one-dimensional. Also, it is likely that performance fluctuations with changing arousal are not gradual as indicated by the inverted-U, but dramatic and in some cases catastrophic, as will be discussed below.

MULTIDIMENSIONAL ANXIETY THEORY

Adopting a multidimensional approach, Martens and colleagues (1990) proposed that cognitive anxiety, somatic anxiety and self-confidence each had different relationships with performance. Performance was predicted to have a negative relationship with cognitive anxiety (increase in cognitive anxiety is associated with decrease in performance). Somatic anxiety was hypothesised to have an inverted-U relationship with performance. Self-confidence was predicted to have a positive relationship with performance (increased self-confidence is associated with improved performance). Along with proposing the multidimensional anxiety theory, Martens also published the Competitive State Anxiety Inventory-2 (CSAI-2) to help researchers test the model's predictions.

Similar to the drive theory and the inverted-U, research evidence has been mixed and the three predictions have not been supported conclusively. One issue is that the model does not account for interactions among somatic anxiety, cognitive anxiety and self-confidence. These constructs are likely to relate to each other in ways that influence performance. The catastrophe model is one theory that examines how the interactions among these variables might influence performance.

THE CATASTROPHE MODEL

The catastrophe model, illustrated in Figure 3.1, predicts interactive relationships between cognitive anxiety, physiological arousal and performance (Hardy and Parfitt 1991). Although seemingly

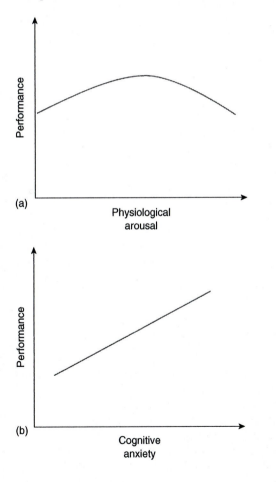

(Continued)

(Continued)

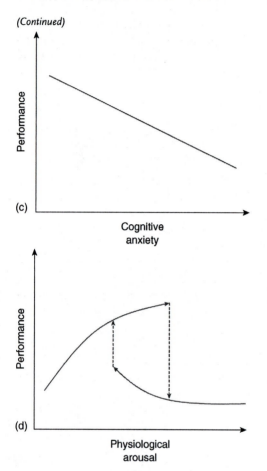

Figure 3.1: The catastrophe model: (a) low cognitive anxiety; (b) low physiological arousal; (c) high physiological arousal; (d) high cognitive anxiety.

complicated, it is best understood by examining each of its components individually. When cognitive anxiety is low, physiological arousal has a flattened inverted-U relationship with performance (Figure 3.1a). When physiological arousal is low, the model predicts a positive relationship between cognitive anxiety and performance: increase in cognitive anxiety leads to an increase in performance (Figure 3.1b). When physiological arousal is high, performance is negatively related with cognitive anxiety: as cognitive anxiety increases incrementally, performance drops gradually (Figure 3.1c). The most dramatic predictions occur when cognitive anxiety is high. At high levels of cognitive anxiety, physiological arousal increases are related to improved performance until reaching the athlete's tolerance or threshold. At this point there is a sudden and catastrophic performance drop to a level below that prior to the experienced catastrophe (Figure 3.1d). When such a catastrophic performance decline has occurred, large decreases in physiological arousal are needed before the athlete can achieve their previously high performance levels.

In addition to the above, the catastrophe model predicts that when physiological arousal and cognitive anxiety are both high, performance will be either dismal or outstanding; that is, hot or cold, but not lukewarm (Figure 3.1d). Also, when cognitive anxiety is high, the same level of physiological arousal may have a different effect on performance depending on whether arousal is increasing towards, or decreasing from, its maximum level. When arousal is increasing, performance will improve (Figure 3.1d). When arousal is decreasing, performance will deteriorate (Figure 3.1d). Although the catastrophe theory is complicated and difficult to test, some initial support has been gathered and it helps account for inconsistencies in previous research. Nevertheless, according to most reviewers more research is needed.

DIRECTIONAL INTERPRETATION HYPOTHESIS

The models presented have focused on how the intensity or level of anxiety and arousal that athletes experience relate to performance. In contrast, Jones, Hanton, Mellalieu and colleagues have argued that to gain an understanding of anxiety and sports performance relationships, both the intensity of athletes' anxieties and their interpretation of their symptoms need to be considered (Hanton and Jones 1999; Mellalieu et al. 2006). Athletes may interpret their anxiety symptoms as facilitative (helpful) or as debilitative (unhelpful) for performance. Although two athletes may experience the same intensity of anxiety, they may perceive its effects on performance differently, and it is these interpretations, rather than the intensity, that are most influential for performance. There is some evidence that athletes who interpret their anxieties as facilitative have greater self-confidence, are more resilient, cope more effectively with obstacles and perform better than individuals who interpret their nerves as debilitative. It also seems possible to teach people how to have facilitative rather than debilitative interpretations (see some example strategies below).

The directional hypothesis has been challenged, however, on a number of grounds. For example, if anxiety is defined as the perception of threat, and athletes are interpreting their symptoms positively or as indicating they are ready to perform, then are they really experiencing anxiety? Related to this, given the current psychological assessment tools, it is difficult to measure separately athletes' anxiety levels, their perceptions of those levels, their perceptions of how those levels influence performance and the actual effect those levels have on performance. Despite these difficulties, the directional hypothesis highlights how different interpretations of arousal can influence athletes' perceptions and performance, an idea that may stimulate ways to help athletes (see below for examples).

CONSCIOUS PROCESSING HYPOTHESIS

The models above are typically descriptive and do not explain why anxiety might influence performance. The conscious processing hypothesis is an example of a model that seeks to provide an explanation for how anxiety may interrupt performance (Masters and Maxwell 2008). As individuals become skilled at a task, they are able to perform automatically and can focus their attention elsewhere. Driving provides an often-cited example of the automation process. Beginner drivers need to coach themselves through the task as they attempt to coordinate their use of the clutch, brake, accelerator and gear stick, while at the same time keeping their eyes on the road. With experience, driving becomes automatic, and people are able to engage in other activities, such as holding conversations, changing radio stations and drinking coffee, while still travelling. Such automation of skill contributes to athletes attaining high levels of performance. For example, elite cricket batters may experience playing a shot automatically without realising they have reacted to the bowler. In team sports, players may react to opponents and interact with teammates instinctively without consciously planning their actions. According to conscious processing hypothesis, anxiety may lead people to assume conscious control over automated movements, triggering disruptions in coordination and deterioration in movement. A golfer, for example, approaching the last few holes of a round may realise she has the opportunity to win a club competition and respond with heightened anxiety. The danger, according to conscious processing hypothesis, is that her anxiety may trigger attempts to focus on particular aspects of the swing, such as those her coach recently emphasised, disrupting her coordination and leading to poor performance, a phenomenon sometimes labelled 'paralysis by analysis'.

WHAT ARE THE IMPLICATIONS FROM THE COMMON THEORIES?

Athletes and coaches may wonder what can be learned from the various theories described above if there is mixed evidence for each. Each model, however, contributes to the understanding of the relationships among arousal, anxiety and performance, and together they provide some basis for developing applied strategies, such as those presented at the end of the chapter. These models, for example, highlight that arousal and anxiety are multidimensional and have cognitive, physical and behavioural components. Explanations, models, theories, or interventions are unlikely to be accurate or helpful if they treat arousal and anxiety as one-dimensional constructs.

Athletes' interpretations of their arousal and anxiety symptoms are just as, if not more, influential on their performance than the intensity of the cues. Butterflies in the stomach may be interpreted as a sign that something could go wrong or that the athlete is underprepared, but they might also be a signal that the individual is keen and motivated. Given the role of perception and interpretation, helping athletes develop their self-confidence and teaching them strategies to interpret their bodily signals as positive may help them manage those symptoms. As a related implication, athletes who develop their self-awareness and are able to monitor their bodily states, feelings and emotions are able to make accurate interpretations of their arousal and anxiety, along with the possible consequences.

The effect that anxiety has on performance is not necessarily negative. Sometimes anxiety can influence performance positively. Athletes often report that they do not want to start a sporting event completely anxiety-free and with no arousal, because it would mean they were not bothered with the event. Some level of anxiety or arousal appears to have value for enhancing performance. Similarly, anxiety can be a signal that the athlete has some limitation they need to overcome, rather than avoid, before achieving a higher level of skill at the sport. For example, a rugby league player who realises that his pre-game anxiety is due to a fear that he will be hurt by stronger opponents might use this information to help him engage in resistance training to develop his strength.

Another reason for developing self-awareness is that optimal levels of anxiety and arousal probably vary with the task being performed and the athlete's personal characteristics. Athletes who are able to recognise the levels of anxiety at which they perform their best in their sports are able to use strategies to manage their emotions to increase the likelihood they will perform to their potential.

THE STRESS PROCESS

Earlier, stress was defined as a perceived imbalance between what is being asked of an athlete and the person's ability to cope with those demands, where failure has severe consequences. One way to understand stress is to view it as a process, and McGrath (1970) developed a four-stage model to explain why stress may hinder performance. In stage 1, athletes are subjected to objective demands. The objective demands placed on a female triathlete include, for example, the course, the condition and the other contestants. To win the event, she has to complete the course faster than the time set by the quickest opponent.

Stage 2 involves the triathlete's interpretation of these objective demands. The triathlete may perceive the situation as nonthreatening either because she believes that she has sufficient skill and physical conditioning to win the race or because the consequences of failure do not upset her. For example, if the person entered the race for enjoyment and was primarily focused on doing as well as she could and perhaps attaining a new personal best, then she could still achieve these aims without having to win. Alternatively, if winning the race was needed for her to be selected to represent her country at an international championship, a goal that she was desperate to achieve, and her training had been compromised by illness, then she may be more likely to perceive an imbalance between her skill and the task demands. The perception of threat will also be influenced by individual differences among athletes. Two athletes, for example, who have the same ability levels, who are experiencing the same task demands, and who are facing the same consequences of failure, may still differ in their stress response if they have different levels of competitive trait anxiety. The person with the higher trait anxiety levels will likely perceive a greater imbalance and respond with greater stress.

Stage 3 involves the response to the perceived imbalance. If the triathlete perceived a substantial imbalance between the task demands and her skill, and the consequences of failure upset her, then she would probably react with high levels of arousal and state anxiety, both cognitive and somatic. Accompanying these reactions would be muscle tension and disruptions to her attention and concentration. Elevated muscle tension may lead to uncoordinated movement and hindered skill execution. Poor coordination may impair her movement economy, causing her to fatigue and not be able to complete the course as fast as expected. In addition, as arousal increases, an athlete's attention field narrows. If the triathlete's attention field narrows too far then she may miss important cues such as where her opponents are or mile markers during the cycle and run stages. Also, the athlete may focus on irrelevant or distracting thoughts that do not help her perform. One such example occurs when athletes notice they are stressed and then begin to worry about their worries. In these cases anxiety can quickly spiral out of control, the athlete chokes and a performance catastrophe occurs.

Behavioural consequences are the focus on stage 4, and these refer to performance and competitive outcomes. The triathlete may record a slow time and her final placing may be lower than it would have been if she had had a different interpretation of the objective demands. Understanding the stress process is useful because it highlights areas, or points of leverage, where sport psychologists might be able to help athletes. They might help the athlete reduce the potential for an imbalance between task demands and athlete capabilities, change athletes' perceptions, or teach clients ways to manage their reactions.

STRESS SOURCES

Sport psychologists have asked athletes about the events, people and things that they find stressful. Paralleling the discussion on anxiety, any aspect about competition that results in a perceived imbalance between task demands and skills can be classified as a source of stress. Researchers have found various stress sources including inter- and intrapersonal factors. Other people represent one source of stress, such as teammates, coaches, family members, officials and spectators. These people may place undue expectations on athletes or make life difficult. Conflicts or disagreements with other people may lead athletes to doubt their ability to cope with their sporting demands. Also, athletes' own anxieties and doubts can trigger stress and they may start to worry about worrying. Another intrapersonal source of stress includes athletes' perceptions about their readiness for sport. They may question whether they have the physical, technical or psychological capacity to perform, leading to thoughts about failure. During performance, mistakes, fatigue or playing below expectations may also trigger stress. In addition to inter- and intra-personal variables that cause athletes to doubt their competence, dimensions of the event or the environment may raise doubts. Lack of funding, inadequate equipment, poor playing or weather conditions, tough opponents, etc. may elicit stress.

A common reason why these sources trigger stress is because they threaten athletes' ability to convey to others and themselves positive images of being skilled, fit, competent, etc. (James and Collins 1997). In sport, athletes are aware that valued others (e.g. coaches, spectators, teammates) may evaluate them positively or negatively. According to impression management theory (Leary 1992), people are motivated to portray themselves in a positive light (a) for social and material reasons (e.g. to be selected as team captain); (b) to reinforce their self-image (e.g. if valued others think they are skilled then they may be more likely to think they are talented); and (c) to help manage their emotions (similar to the adage that if those who act confident become confident). Competitive stress results when athletes are highly motivated to manage their image but doubt they can do so. For example, a lack of preparation may lead to an athlete becoming stressed because she wants to look good to the coach in training so as to get selected for the following game.

WAYS SPORT PSYCHOLOGISTS HELP ATHLETES MANAGE THEIR ANXIETIES AND STRESS

Recalling the case story that opened this chapter, Coach Beckmann could reflect on the stress process to identify ways to help Chuck. One strategy is to reduce the potential for an imbalance between perceived task demands and athlete capabilities by developing a structured training plan through which Chuck will improve his skill and physical conditioning. Increasing his skill level, as long as he is aware of his improvement, will reduce the possibility that Chuck perceives that he is out of his depth. Simulation training may also help Chuck prepare for competition. In simulation training, Coach Beckmann would attempt to recreate a competition as closely as possible to the real thing during a practice session. Chuck might then become comfortable having to perform under pressure.

Coach Beckmann could also assist Chuck by helping him to reduce the perceived consequences of failure. In Chuck's case, he was worried that failure indicated he was not good at something he valued and that he was not able to come through for a friend. She might explain to Chuck that his ability at the sport is just one factor of several that influence judges' decisions and they have a short time to assess several couples in any one dance. Also, the presence of other good dancers on the floor does not mean that he is not a skilled athlete; instead, being on the floor suggests he has some skill. Taken together, a poor placing in a competition is insufficient evidence to conclude he is without skill at something he values. Also, she could explain that 'it takes two to tango' and ask him what advice he would give Sarah if she expressed the same worry about not delivering for a friend. Chuck could then try to apply the same advice himself to cope with his fear. Some consoling words from Sarah might further help to reduce the perceived consequences.

As a third series of strategies, Coach Beckmann, or a sport psychologist, might teach Chuck ways to manage his emotions and reactions before, during and after competition. In Chapter 7, common strategies used by sport psychologists, such as goal-setting, imagery, self-talk and relaxation, are discussed as part of psychological skills training programmes. These interventions may be used to help athletes accept, control, reduce and possibly eliminate anxieties, worries and stress. Relaxation techniques, for example, might allow Chuck to reduce his feelings of nervousness. Self-talk may help him to direct his attention to useful task-relevant thoughts or even alter his perceptions so they are facilitative rather than debilitative.

Another way that these strategies can assist Chuck is by helping him develop his confidence. In some ways self-confidence is the antithesis of anxiety. Anxiety involves the perception that 'I might fail here and that will hurt me in some (physical or psychological) way', whereas self-confidence involves thinking that 'I can do well here'. It would seem that helping Chuck develop his self-belief might buffer or protect him from experiencing anxiety in future competitions. In the next chapter I focus on sport psychologists' understanding of self-confidence in sport.

REFERENCES

Hanton, S. and Jones, G. (1999). The effects of a multimodal intervention program on performers: II. Training the butterflies to fly in formation. *The Sport Psychologist, 13*, 22–41.

Hardy, L. and Parfitt, G. (1991). A catastrophe model of anxiety and performance. *British Journal of Psychology, 82*, 163–178.

James, B. and Collins, D. (1997). Self-presentational sources of competitive stress during performance. *Journal of Sport & Exercise Psychology, 19*, 17–35.

Leary, M. R. (1992). Self-presentational processes in exercise and sport. *Journal of Sport & Exercise Psychology, 14*, 339–351.

Martens, R., Vealey, R. S. and Burton, D. (1990). *Competitive anxiety in sport.* Champaign, IL: Human Kinetics.

Masters, R. and Maxwell,, J. (2008). The theory of reinvestment. *International Review of Sport and Exercise Psychology, 1*, 160–183.

McGrath, J. E. (1970). Major methodological issues. In J. E. McGrath (Ed.), *Social and psychological factors in stress* (pp. 19–49). New York: Holt, Rinehart & Winston.

Mellalieu, S. D., Hanton, S. and Fletcher, D. (2006). A competitive anxiety review: Recent directions in sport psychology research. In S. Hanton and S. D. Mellalieu (Eds), *Literature reviews in sport psychology* (pp. 1–45). New York: Nova Science.

Moran, A. P. (2012). *Sport and exercise psychology: A critical introduction*. London: Routledge.

Uphill, M. (2008). Anxiety in sport: Should we be worried or excited? In A. Lane (Ed.), *Sport and exercise psychology: Topics in applied psychology* (pp. 35–51). London: Hodder Education.

4

SELF-CONFIDENCE

CHAPTER LEARNING OUTCOMES

1 Define self-confidence.
2 Overview the major theories for understanding self-confidence.
3 Depict the relationship between self-confidence and sport performance.
4 Illustrate how self-confidence might be enhanced.

John and Chris were best friends who were also seniors playing for Sacred Heart High School's basketball team. Although the two were close buddies and had grown up together, they were completely different during a game. Chris brimmed with confidence; in any pressure situation he told Coach Cox that he wanted to be on the court and that he would win the game for the team. In contrast, when under pressure or stressed, John appeared to freeze up and would make mistakes. Coach Cox often felt like he had to take John off the court for his own and the team's benefit. Coach was an excitable character who sometimes let his emotions get the better of him. On a few occasions he lost his cool and would accidently say something he would later regret. For example, one time Coach Cox became frustrated and told John that he was a lame excuse for a player who was no better than a rabbit caught in a car's headlights, although he apologised later. When Coach spoke to John about why he often froze during competition, John replied saying he did not know why, but just didn't think he was capable of coming through for the team when it counted. As much as Coach Cox found it hard to help John, he also wished he could take some of Chris's confidence and inject it into John. Sometimes Coach thought Chris was overconfident, particularly when playing against weak opponents. In these situations, Chris was a slow starter, acting like he was not bothered with the game. Such an attitude seemed infectious, and in two games, the team had almost let the opposition get too far ahead on the scoreboard before upping the intensity of the game and coming from behind to win. Coach Cox decided to ask Molly Clock, the school's counselling psychologist if she has any ideas for helping John.

Athletes, coaches and fans have strong beliefs about the role of confidence in sports performance. When asked about the psychological ingredients that contribute to good performance, athletes or coaches almost universally include self-confidence in their lists. Furthermore, journalists and spectators typically describe elite and successful athletes as being supremely confident. They may also attribute poor performance to a loss of confidence. Nevertheless, elite athletes experience self-doubts on occasion. It is possible, however, that athletes can still perform successfully while having doubts and anxieties (see Chapter 3 on arousal, anxiety and stress). Given the large number of factors that influence athletic performance, it is understandable that high self-confidence may not always be necessary for successful performance. Often athletes also suggest that self-doubts can be helpful by increasing their motivation, refocusing their attention to the task at hand, or helping them identify weaknesses they then strive to overcome. Potentially, a drop in confidence might lead to increased performance either immediately or over time. The relationship between confidence and performance appears to be more complicated than the assumption that 'more is better'. Sport psychologists have conducted a great deal of research on the role of confidence in sport, and in this chapter I define confidence; describe two of the dominant theories practitioners use to understand self-confidence;

explore the relationship between self-confidence and sport performance, behaviour, emotions and cognitions; and discuss ways to increase self-confidence.

WHAT IS SELF-CONFIDENCE?

Self-confidence focuses on athletes' perceptions about their abilities to achieve success. A gymnast with high levels of self-confidence, for example, believes she has the technical skill, strength and stamina to perform her routines and attain high scores. Similar to other psychological constructs, self-confidence can be viewed from a trait-like or state-like perspective. From a state-like view, confidence refers to athletes' perceptions about their abilities to achieve success at the current moment. As such, athletes' levels in state confidence are likely to fluctuate over time as their perceptions about the situation and their abilities to meet the demands placed on them change. State-like confidence is also likely to be influenced by trait-like beliefs. Trait self-confidence refers to athletes' usual or typical beliefs about their chances of succeeding at their sport. Measures of trait self-confidence should vary less on a moment-by-moment basis compared with state assessments. The trait and state self-confidence distinction can help explain why elite athletes can have high levels of self-beliefs but also experience self-doubts from time to time. Also, the division helps us understand why elite athletes can bounce back from or use their self-doubts to enhance their focus, increase their motivation, or develop their skill. Much research on self-confidence in sport psychology has been informed by Albert Bandura's (1997) self-efficacy theory and Vealey's (2001) model of sport confidence. As such, it is useful to discuss these two approaches.

BANDURA'S SELF-EFFICACY THEORY

Self-efficacy refers to athletes' beliefs that they can execute the behaviours required to produce desired outcomes, and they are distinct from outcome expectations, which involve beliefs that certain actions lead to specific consequences. For example, a javelin thrower might believe he is able to execute the correct technique and attain a certain distance. His outcome expectation is that the distance will result in him winning a competition. Both self-efficacy and outcome expectations influence behaviour and performance. Athletes who do not believe a desired outcome will result from a specific behaviour (low outcome expectancy) may be less motivated to try or persist in those actions. Even if they do think a specific behaviour will result in a desired outcome, they may still lack motivation if they doubt their ability to perform that behaviour (low self-efficacy).

There are three dimensions along which self-efficacy can vary, including level, generality and strength. Level refers to the standard of performance athletes believe they can achieve or the degree of difficulty they perceive they can surmount. For example, Chris from the opening case example might be confident he could achieve eight out of ten attempts at the free throw line, whereas John might believe he could only get two out of ten attempts. Regarding generality, people may view themselves as capable across a range of domains (e.g. sport, education and career) or only in a small number of areas of functioning. Generality also varies across types of activities, capability modality (e.g. thinking, emotion and behaviour), different situations and the types of people with which athletes interact. For example, a hockey player might believe she can play well both defensively and offensively in an upcoming game. Her self-efficacy, however, might vary depending on the type of surface she will play on (natural or artificial turf) or the opposition the team is up against.

Self-efficacy also varies in strength. Weak self-efficacy is easily negated by disconfirming experiences, whereas people with strong self-efficacy have tenacious beliefs in their abilities and typically persevere in their efforts despite difficulties and obstacles. These athletes are not put off by adversity. Self-efficacy strength is not related to choices athletes make about what tasks to attempt in a straightforward way. A minimum threshold of self-efficacy is needed before they will initiate an attempt, but stronger levels of self-assurance result in the same behaviours. Stronger self-efficacy, however, leads to greater perseverance and likelihood that the chosen activity will be performed successfully.

In addition to self-efficacy, motivation and ability influence behaviour and performance. According to Bandura's theory, when athletes have the physical capacity, skills and the desire, their self-efficacy will be a major predictor of their performance. Self-efficacy influences athletes' performance through their behaviours, thoughts and emotions. Lacrosse players, for instance, with high self-efficacy will likely choose to attend training regularly, expend high levels of effort, and persist longer than those with low self-beliefs. These self-efficacious individuals will set higher goals and have more helpful thoughts and emotions. As a result, they may have a better chance of success.

According to Bandura, athletes' self-efficacy beliefs are constructed from four major sources: mastery experiences; vicarious experiences; verbal persuasion; and physiological and emotional states. These four sources can enhance or deflate self-efficacy. In ice hockey, for example, players on the bench watching teammates performing well against opponents may experience enhanced self-efficacy. Alternatively, these individuals' self-efficacy may drop if they observe teammates struggling. These sources, however, do not automatically change self-efficacy, but only when athletes interpret the information associated with that source. Benched ice hockey players' self-efficacies may not improve when observing teammates performing well if they think their teammates are much more skilled than themselves.

- *Mastery experiences* have more influence on self-efficacy than the other three below. Having completed a task previously provides the most authentic evidence that an individual can be successful. Previous success may enhance self-efficacy, whereas past failures may reduce self-belief. Nevertheless, previous successes and failures do not necessarily influence self-efficacy if athletes attribute outcomes to other causes. Most people realise that sports performance is influenced by various factors, such as the opponents, circumstances surrounding the events (e.g. weather, surface conditions, crowd support) and officials' decisions. Athletes' interpretations of these factors influence whether previous performances influence self-efficacy. A sprinter who achieved a personal best in a recent competition may not have enhanced self-efficacy in an upcoming race if she thought her time was wind assisted.
- *Vicarious experiences* refer to watching other people perform an activity. The person might be performing the task live or on a screen. Self-modelling occurs when athletes view themselves

performing, such as when coaches film their athletes for instructional purposes. Self-modelling also includes imagery, a technique sport psychologists commonly use when working with athletes (and is discussed in Chapter 7). Individuals' interpretations of the demonstration have a bearing on the influences that observing a model has on self-efficacy. The type of model used may influence the change in self-efficacy. Demonstrations may be more influential when the athlete and model are similar in ability and other personal attributes. Observing multiple models may be more helpful than watching a single person.

- *Verbal persuasion* occurs when other people express their belief in athletes' capabilities, such as when teammates talk each other up for an event. Verbal persuasion can lead to improved self-efficacy if realistic, but may not result in lasting improvement when used alone. Nevertheless, verbal persuasion might improve self-efficacy enough so that individuals persist until they succeed and then mastery experiences may enhance self-efficacy further. When the exhortations come from another person, then athletes' perceptions of persuaders' credibility and knowledge of the activity will influence verbal persuasion's effectiveness to increase self-efficacy. Athletes may believe the words of highly respected, experienced coaches, for example, more than unknown spectators.

- *Physiological and emotional states* provide clues regarding athletes' abilities to meet task demands successfully. People who get tired walking, for example, may doubt they can complete a 5 km fun run. Netball players who observe they are uptight and have jittery stomachs prior to a game may expect to make mistakes and perform poorly. Similar to the other three information sources discussed above, actual physiological and emotional states do not influence self-efficacy. Instead, athletes' interpretations of their states influence their self-efficacy.

In any situation athletes may be receive information from multiple sources and each may have a different effect on self-efficacy. Also, athletes may vary in their responses to the sources and interpret them differently. Coaches will find their attempts to build self-efficacy more successful if they consider how athletes are likely to react to their interventions. In the opening case story,

Coach Cox may need to talk to John and Chris in different ways to achieve the same result – high self-efficacy.

VEALEY'S MODEL OF SPORT CONFIDENCE

Based on Bandura's self-efficacy theory, Vealey developed a model of self-confidence focused on sport. In her model, sport confidence refers to the level of certainty athletes have about their abilities to achieve success in sport. A baseball pitcher with high levels of self-confidence, for example, may believe he can throw the perfect game against an upcoming opponent. For Vealey, as discussed above, sport confidence can be both state-like and trait-like. An athlete's belief about a specific task or event at a particular moment in time is an expression of state confidence. Trait sport confidence refers to an athlete's typical level of certainty about their ability to succeed across time.

Vealey's model is presented in Figure 4.1; she argued that the culture within a sporting organisation influences how athletes' confidence is developed and manifested. For example, in a professional team with a long history of success, young recruits may believe they are in a good position to develop their skills and build lucrative careers (these athletes' confidence is influenced by situational favourableness). In a struggling team with high player turnover and frequent coaching changes, new recruits

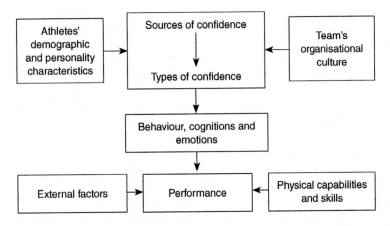

Figure 4.1: Vealey's model of sport confidence.

may be unsure if they are going to be nurtured. Vealey's model also indicates that demographic (e.g. age, gender) and personality differences among individuals influences the display and development of sport confidence. For example, older athletes may believe that they not able to maintain the intensity of younger athletes and may experience lowered confidence.

There are different domains of sport confidence in the model, including resilience, physical skills and training and cognitive efficiency. Resilience refers to athletes' beliefs they can regain focus, recover from poor performances, resolve doubts and overcome setbacks. Physical skills and training refers to athletes' beliefs in their abilities to execute the physical skills and movements needed for successful performance. Cognitive efficiency refers to how certain athletes are that they can focus, maintain concentration and make suitable decisions.

Whereas there were four sources of self-efficacy in Bandura's model, Vealey identified a greater range of influences on sport confidence. Athletes' sport confidence will increase when they: (a) perceive they are mastering the demands of the sport (mastery); (b) demonstrate high levels of skill (ability demonstration); (c) observe models performing well (vicarious experiences); (d) think others are supportive and encouraging (social support), (e) believe in their coach's leadership abilities (coach leadership); (f) feel mentally and physically prepared (preparation); (g) think they appear well to others (physical self-presentation; (h) think the situation favours them (situational favourableness);and (i) feel comfortable in the environment (environmental comfort). Understanding the sources that enhance sport confidence will help athletes and coaches identify ways to build confidence and perhaps enhance performance.

Vealey described sport confidence as a 'mental modifier' that influences how athletes feel, think, behave and perform. Although confidence may lead to helpful emotions, behaviours and thoughts, Vealey acknowledged that sometimes athletes' performances are hindered or enhanced by factors outside their control (e.g. weather, luck or opponents), or because they do not have the necessary physical skills and capabilities to complete a task successfully.

There are similarities between Bandura's and Vealey's models that help reinforce some keys aspects regarding confidence, and also have applied implications that will be presented later in the chapter. Both models define confidence (and self-efficacy) as being multidimensional, varying in terms of strength and specificity. Also, levels of self-assurance are influenced by various sources that are internal and external to athletes. Self-belief is not something that athletes are born with or without, but is a mind-set that fluctuates as individuals encounter different situations and build up a personal life history. Coaches and athletes can identify ways to boost confidence levels to gain the potential benefits in terms of persistence, adaptive cognitions and performance. As a third similarity, although both models argue that self-belief influences performance, they acknowledge that confidence is one of many factors that contribute to goal achievement in sport. Sometimes overeager pop psychologists argue that a high level of confidence is sufficient for performance success, and they bandy around catch phrases such as 'what the mind can conceive and believe, the body will achieve'. Bandura and Vealey remind us that sporting success depends of many factors, some of which are within athletes' control and some that are not.

SELF-CONFIDENCE AND SPORT PERFORMANCE

Sport psychologists have conducted a large number of studies examining the relationship between self-confidence and performance. To interpret the research, it is helpful to recall the differentiation between descriptive and experimental research discussed in the Introduction to the book. In descriptive research, sport psychologists measure athletes' self-confidence (e.g. through a questionnaire) and their performance (e.g. sprint time). They then work out if the two measures vary together; that is, do people who get high confidence scores also perform better than those who score less on the questionnaire. Although descriptive research indicates if confidence is related to performance, it cannot tell you if confidence caused performance. Maybe performance caused confidence. Maybe another variable that was unmeasured caused both and the relationship between confidence and performance is just an artefact of the study's design. Experimental research provides clues as to whether confidence influences performance. In experimental studies, investigators manipulate confidence to see if performance changes. If performance varies with the manipulated changes in confidence (performance increases when athletes are helped to have high confidence but drops when confidence is lowered) then there is some evidence that confidence causes performance.

From descriptive research it is clear that athletes and coaches believe self-confidence contributes to sporting success. When asked, athletes and coaches almost always list self-belief or confidence as one of the characteristics of elite performance and sports people. A second finding is that self-confidence does vary with different measures of performance or athletic level. Elite athletes report higher levels of self-confidence than non-elite athletes. As a third finding, measures of self-confidence taken before a competitive event are related, albeit weakly, to performance. Although in such cases performance cannot have caused self-confidence, there is still the possibility that another variable influenced both. As one example, sport psychologists have found that the confidence–performance relationship is influenced by task familiarity. Athletes who are familiar with a task may well be more confident and also better skilled than those people unaccustomed with the sport. It is their higher skill level that may lead to better performance.

Although it is generally not possible to conclude from descriptive research that self-confidence influences performance, sport psychologists have conducted some experiments revealing that self-confidence may be a causal factor in sport skill execution. In a classic study, Nelson and Furst (1972) had 12 pairs of participants arm-wrestle each other when both contestants believed the weaker individual to be the stronger person. In 10 of the 12 pairs, the winner was the person who was objectively weaker, but thought to be stronger by both participants. These results, which have been supported by other studies since, parallel the views of most athletes and coaches, that people's expectations have an influence on performance.

A related belief regarding self-confidence among athletes and coaches is the notion of psychological momentum, or the idea that success breeds success. Sport psychologists have attempted to examine psychological momentum, and this work is presented in Box 4.1.

BOX 4.1: **DOES CONFIDENCE HELP ATHLETES GET ON A ROLL?**

A belief among many sports-minded people is that 'success breeds success' or the suggestion that players who experience positive performance outcomes are more likely to continue being successful than if they have a series of failures. As an example, some people perceive that players who score a run of baskets early in a basketball game will get on to a hot streak and will be more successful for the rest of the game than if they miss their early attempts. An increase in confidence is one of the common reasons athletes and spectators offer to explain this phenomenon. Early success increases players' self-beliefs which in turn influence subsequent performance allowing for greater improvements in confidence and so on, leading to a spiral of confidence-fuelled success. Also, people may believe in a spiral of failure where one mistake or poor performance leads to another through the lowering of confidence. Although sport psychologists are not immune to such perceptions, some researchers have sought to examine this idea with a view to identifying if it is replicable and if there are ways to help athletes trigger a run of success.

These researchers have formalised these ideas under the label of psychological momentum (Crust and Nesti 2006). Although researchers have examined psychological momentum in sport for more than 30 years there is still debate over what it is, whether it is real or illusionary and the causes if it does exist. Broadly, the various descriptions of momentum propose that some event, typically a physical one, triggers changes in athletes' confidence (motivation, attention, etc.) that influence their persistence, effort or skill level and ultimately performance outcome. These triggers may often be labelled as game-changing plays. In rugby union, for example, a spark of brilliance leading to a try or a thumping tackle that leaves an opposition attack dead in the water helps a player or team realise that they have the ability to do well and so increase the intensity of their game, eventually overpowering the opposition. Equally, the inability to score after a period of sustained attack may leave players dejected and despairing of being able to compete successfully. Such perceptions of impending doom lead to a withdrawal of effort.

Investigators have used two main research approaches to examine psychological momentum. First, they have used observational or archival data from sporting events to see if performance increases after a hot streak. A recent meta-analysis of 30 studies revealed no evidence that a 'hot hand' exists in sport: (a) generally; (b) for teams or individuals; (c) within or across games; or (d) for team or individual sports (Avugos *et al.* 2013). As the second main approach, sport psychologists have conducted experiments in which they have given athletes false feedback or used different scoring manipulations to change athletes' perceptions regarding psychological momentum. Results from these studies have been inconsistent, with some positive and some negative results, although they have also often been criticised for having weaknesses that limit the ability to interpret the results unambiguously. Both avenues of research do not provide convincing evidence for the existence of psychological momentum. In light of the difficulties sport psychologists have had in demonstrating the existence of psychological momentum in sport, it is unsurprising that they have also not often considered the reasons for any effect. Even if psychological momentum does exist, it is still an open question regarding the role of confidence (or any other variable) in causing the phenomenon. Nevertheless, the notion of psychological momentum and game-changing events is appealing and likely to continue to be alluring to sports fans, athletes and coaches as an intuitive explanation for what they observe in sport.

Increasing self-confidence can sometimes also lead to a drop in performance (Woodman *et al.* 2010). If high self-confidence, for example, leads athletes to reduce their effort, allow their minds to wander off task or engage in unnecessary risks, then their performance may decrease. Bandura (1997) has suggested that some level of self-doubt can be beneficial and may provide the incentive to rally together the resources needed to master the task. In the chapter's opening vignette, Chris appears to be an athlete, who on occasion, might benefit from some doubt or uncertainty about the result to help him work towards achieving optimal performance.

SELF-CONFIDENCE, BEHAVIOURS, COGNITIONS AND EMOTIONS

Knowing that self-confidence can influence performance begs the question, why? The possible reasons focus on behaviour, cognitions and emotions. First, the existing evidence indicates that athletes with higher levels of confidence or self-efficacy exert more effort, persist longer and select more difficult tasks when performing, compared with individuals with lower self-beliefs. Individuals who select difficult tasks, expend lots of effort and persist in their attempts, probably improve their skill levels more and attain higher levels of sporting success than individuals who choose easy activities and who do not persevere. Second, self-confidence is related to various thoughts, perceptions and beliefs that may influence performance, including perceived ability, self-esteem, sport identity, competitiveness, goal commitment, a focus on self-improvement, concentration and effective decision-making. It might be expected that confident individuals, compared with those who doubt their abilities, may have the positive self-perceptions and adaptive achievement-related beliefs that contribute to enhanced performance. Third, self-confidence increases as positive moods and emotions improve and decreases as negative moods and emotion intensify. Also self-confidence may buffer the influence of anxiety on performance. Taken together, these results may indicate that self-confident athletes develop higher levels of skill and the mind-set that allows them to perform better than less confident sports participants.

ENHANCING SELF-CONFIDENCE

Kurt Lewin, a famous psychologist, once said 'There is nothing so practical as a good theory,' and his words are applicable to enhancing confidence in athletes. Based on Bandura's and Vealey's models, it is possible to generate practical strategies that can help enhance athletes' self-confidence (Short and Ross-Stewart 2009). Bandura's four sources of self-efficacy, for example, can help identify strategies that Coach Cox above could use to build John's confidence.

With respect to mastery, Coach Cox could structure the practice environment to focus on progressive skill development. Increased skill level will allow John to feel prepared for competition. Coach could also make use of simulation training in which he recreates as much as possible the circumstances that arise during basketball, such as having to make shots at the free throw line to win a game. Increasing John's familiarity with the types of situations he encounters will encourage him to believe that he can cope. These strategies will help build John's confidence if he experiences success in coping with the situations and his skill levels improve (otherwise his self-efficacy may drop). The strategies will be less helpful if John repeatedly does not cope and his skill levels remain the same. To help ensure success and skill development, Coach Cox could employ goal-setting to identify a realistic series of targets and goal achievement strategies (see Chapter 7 for more detail about goal-setting).

Based on evidence that vicarious experiences can increase self-confidence, Coach Cox could use live and recorded demonstrations to help John develop a mental picture in which he sees himself performing well. Although there are numerous videos of elite basketball players freely available on in the internet via sites such as YouTube, Coach Cox might find that John does not respond to such videos with increased self-confidence, but instead suggests he has no chance of ever reaching that level of skill. Instead, using recordings of John's friend Chris and other teammates might be effective in building self-efficacy because they may better demonstrate a realistic achievable level of skill. The effectiveness of these recordings may be enhanced if the models demonstrate high levels of self-belief. Also, recordings of John coping well with game-specific situations are likely to be effective as well.

As an additional strategy under the vicarious experience umbrella, imagery is a technique in which athletes imagine themselves coping with the demands of their sport. With regards to self-efficacy, imagery is another way that John could develop a mental picture of himself as a capable, confident, developing athlete. Just as positive imagery can enhance self-efficacy, negative images, where John views himself performing poorly, can reduce his beliefs in his ability. Details about how imagery might be used effectively are presented in Chapter 7.

Coach Cox can develop strategies to help John based on Bandura's third self-efficacy source category, verbal persuasion. The role of verbal persuasion can help Coach Cox understand why his outburst dismissing John as a lame excuse for a player, no better than a stunned rabbit, was unlikely to be helpful. He was communicating that he had no confidence in John. It would understandable if John reacted by thinking 'if coach has no confidence and he knows what he is talking about, why should I believe I can improve?' Normally, focusing on players' capabilities and outlining how they can develop will build self-efficacy better than focusing on their deficiencies or limitations. Just like using role models who can provide a realistic standard of performance to which John can aspire, Coach Cox's attempts at verbal persuasion will yield benefits if he uses believable statements. One way is to separate outcome from performance. By focusing on what John can control (i.e. his performance), Coach Cox's verbal persuasion can be more realistic than when emphasising things over which complete control is not always possible (i.e. winning or losing).

Self-talk is a strategy in which athletes verbally direct their attention to those thoughts they want to have rather than letting their minds wander and potentially resulting in unhelpful or irrelevant inner dialogue. Coach Cox could help John enhance his self-efficacy by teaching him some self-talk strategies to focus on what he is capable of attaining and reminding himself of his existing skills and achievements. Suggestions that could help Coach Cox are presented in Chapter 7 where self-talk is discussed in greater detail.

There are two types of strategies that Coach Cox can use that would address the physiological and emotional states category in Bandura's model. Coach could help John reinterpret physiological cues and feelings as signs of desire and readiness rather than as anxiety and fear. A second strategy is to teach John methods for regulating his emotional and physiological states. Typically in sport, it is more common for athletes to need to relax and reduce, rather than increase, their arousal levels. There are various techniques that sport psychologists can teach athletes to help them reduce arousal and manage negative emotions and anxieties, such as centring, self-talk and imagery. Again, Chapter 7 details some common strategies.

Coach could also draw on Vealey's model to create additional strategies. According to Vealey, for example, coach leadership and supportive environments foster self-confidence. Developing a cohesive group in which Coach and the players are focused on a common goal and want to help each other may allow John to feel he belongs and that his teammates believe in him. Thinking that those around in him believe in him may enhance his belief in himself.

Coach Cox's attempts to increase self-confidence will probably be more successful if he uses several strategies rather than one. For example, Coach might set John realistic goals focused on skill improvement (mastery), periodically point out how he has improved (verbal persuasion), encourage him to use self-talk (verbal encouragement), film him doing well in competition (vicarious experience) and teach him a relaxation technique to allow him to control his anxieties (physiological and emotional states). Making use of multiple ways to get across his message increases the likelihood that Coach will communicate in a way to which John responds.

Self-confidence demonstrates how applied sport psychology benefits from a practical theory supported by research. There are various strategies from which Coach Cox can select to help John and he can use them with the expectation that they are likely to help. The theories also signal that John's lack of confidence is influenced as much by the people around him as it is by him alone. Although many coaches and athletes believe self-confidence is a key ingredient to successful performance, they may also think it is something that sports people have or don't have, are born with or lack. Instead, self-confidence is an attribute that fluctuates and athletes' self-expectations can increase or decrease. The implication is that athletes like John can be helped to improve their self-efficacy. It is also possible that even elite athletes can experience a crisis of confidence and sometimes need help to maintain their self-beliefs. Like anxiety and stress management, self-confidence is a common presenting issue when athletes approach sport psychologists. As has been indicated above, Chapter 7 will detail some of the more common strategies that sport psychologists use to improve athletes' self-efficacy.

REFERENCES

Avugos, S., Köppen, J., Czienskowski, U., Raab, M. and Bar-Eli, M. (2013). The 'hot hand' reconsidered: A meta-analytic approach. *Psychology of Sport and Exercise, 14*, 21–27.

Bandura, A. (1997). *Self-efficacy: The exercise of control.* New York: Freeman.

Crust, L. and Nesti, M. (2006). A review of psychological momentum in sports: Why qualitative research is needed. *Athletic Insight: The Online Journal of Sport Psychology, 8*, 1–15.

Nelson, L. R. and Furst, M. L. (1972). An objective study of the effects of expectation on competitive performance. *The Journal of Psychology, 81*, 69–72.

Short, S. and Ross-Stewart, L. (2009). A review of self-efficacy based interventions. In S. D. Mellalieu and S. Hanton (Eds), *Advances in applied sport psychology: A review* (pp. 221–280). London: Routledge.

Vealey, R. S. (2001). Understanding and enhancing self-confidence in athletes. In R. N. Singer, H. A. Hausenblas and C. M. Janelle (Eds), *Handbook of sport psychology* (2nd ed., pp. 550–565). New York: Wiley.

Woodman, T., Akehurst, S., Hardy, L. and Beattie, S. (2010). Self-confidence and performance: A little self-doubt helps. *Psychology of Sport and Exercise, 11*, 467–470.

COMPETITION AND AUDIENCE EFFECTS

Jayne and his wife Kaylee, who head up the Parent Teachers Association at Brownell High School, have attended a staff meeting because they are outraged with a proposal to no longer keep score during sports day and to do away with the house cup (where classes are divided into school 'houses' and compete annually for the house cup). Jayne and Kaylee are worried the proposal reflects a larger educational trend to avoid evaluating children against each other. During the meeting the two teachers leading the proposal, Zoe and Hoban, address the committee and present examples of students who are underachieving and think they are worse than the other students at sports and classroom learning, because they always seem to fail at everything. These students feel bad about themselves and have poor self-worth. In response, Jayne talks about how he thinks the proposed changes are short-sighted because students have to learn that the real world is tough. According to him, the sooner the students learn that life is competitive the better. Avoiding competition denies good students a chance to push themselves and tells others it is alright to coast because life is easy. Jayne describes himself as a successful business man and accredits his success to learning early in life that the world did not care about him and he had to look after himself. The meeting gets heated with both sides using emotive language and accusing the others of not caring about the children. The final speaker is Coach Reynolds, who leads the school's football team, the Browncoats. Reynolds is in a cantankerous mood, because he would rather be preparing for a clash against the Reavers, a local school team. He gruffly declares the proposal is educational namby-pamby, and would make no difference at all, because the students will still compare themselves against each other. Reynolds finishes by saying that the only way to remove competition from sport is to stop playing.

Competition and competitive behaviour is pervasive throughout Western society and appear in almost every domain that includes human interaction, such as sport, business, education and the arts. Competition in the sporting domain is a topic that generates polarised views and leads to competitiveness being viewed as either good or bad. Some people argue that competitive sport helps prepare people for what they will experience in life. According to these people, other domains in life are competitive, and sport helps individuals to learn how to compete and survive in business, education, etc. Other people argue that competition is associated with negative psychological consequences that are best avoided: for example, repeated failure through competition teaches some people that they are 'losers' and leads to reduced self-worth, confidence and esteem. At the extreme end, these opponents attempt to remove competitive elements from sport, such as not keeping score.

These views are typically based on personal experiences and anecdotes. For example, elite athletes are often described as fiercely competitive and their attitude is held up as being one of the reasons for their success. From this observation, people suggest that competition is healthy and helps produce champions. As another example, competition may be blamed for why some people feel bad about themselves: they were unable to successfully compete against others and so learned they were without worth. Alternatively, some athletes may be branded as bad losers or take competition so seriously that they cheat or hurt others in their quests to win a game. A more productive way to discuss the value of competition in sport (and other domains of life) is to apply the scientific process to examine the phenomenon. Given that the competitive element of sport is likely to influence human behaviour, it is understandable that sport psychologists have studied the topic. They have wanted to find out the positive and negative consequences of competition and ways in which it might influence behaviour. Sport psychologists have believed that doing so will allow them to contribute to debates about the value of sport in society and help them assist their clients (e.g. learn ways to manage or interpret competitive situations to cope with anxiety). In this chapter I will define competition, detail how competition can be conceptualised, explore the effect competition has on sports performance, examine if sport can build life skills, review the home field advantage in sport and discuss whether an audience influences athletes' performances.

DEFINING COMPETITION

Competition is often defined in terms of reward distribution. Competition is a social process that occurs when rewards (tangible or intangible) are distributed to people unequally, based on their performance in comparison with that of others participating in the same event. The rugby world cup final is an example of an event that most people would agree is competitive. In contrast, a social game of netball among work colleagues or students during lunchtime may or may not be considered competitive based on the players' interpretation of the situation. Some players may not perceive that any rewards are available and they are not engaging in social comparison. Other players may believe that intangible rewards, such as bragging rights, are on the table and are keen on ensuring they win. The example illustrates that competition has both objective and subjective components, a point developed in the next section.

Sometimes people suggest that they are competing against themselves, such as trying to obtain a personal best in a training session (e.g. trying to lower their time in a training run). According to the definition above, sport psychologists would not consider athletes competing against themselves as an example of competition. Instead, these types of personal challenges are better described as achievement situations (or those in which individuals are striving to master a task or achieve some standard of excellence). A competitive event represents a subset of achievement situations where two or more people or teams are trying to outperform each other to obtain the lion's share of the rewards.

MARTENS' MODEL OF COMPETITION

Figure 5.1 presents Martens' (1975) model (in which competition is detailed as a social comparison process involving four stages), which helps explain why people react differently to the same competitive event. The first stage, the *objective competitive situation*, involves a state of affairs in which athletes' performances are compared with some standard of excellence in the presence of one or more people aware of the comparison. American football is one example and involves opponents on the field interacting with each other: each team provides their opponents with the standard of excellence that must be reached to win the event. Both players and spectators are aware of the comparison. Gymnasts provide each other with the standard of excellence, as scored by the judges, despite not competing against each other at the same time. The word 'objective' highlights that the situation is the same for each competitor. All runners in a 10 km race, for example, have to pass the start line, travel the same distance and cross the finish line.

The second stage, the *subjective competitive situation*, focuses on how athletes perceive, appraise and interpret the objective competitive situation. Prior to a 100 m sprint final, for example, some contestants may perceive the upcoming race as a chance to show

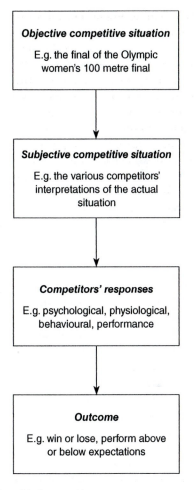

Figure 5.1: Martens' model of competition.

others how talented they are and believe they can win. These individuals are likely to respond differently to those athletes who focus on how spectators might react negatively if they lose and become anxious. Athletes' appraisals are influenced by their personalities, histories, needs and other characteristics, explaining why people interpret the same situation differently to others. Competitive trait anxiety is one athlete factor that influences how people perceive a situation. High-trait-anxious individuals are likely to interpret the objective competitive situation as much more threatening to their psychological and physical well-being compared with low-trait-anxious athletes. Chapters 1–4 detailed various athlete factors (personality, anxiety, motivation and confidence) likely to have a bearing on how athletes appraise and interpret situations.

The ways athletes respond to their interpretations is described in stage 3 of the model. Their interpretations of the objective competitive situation trigger positive or negative adaptions that give athletes greater or lesser chances of performing to expectations. High-trait-anxious athletes, for example, who interpret situations as threatening, are likely to respond with elevated state anxiety and stress levels compared with low-trait-anxious individuals. Athletes' responses may be examined at the psychological, physiological and behavioural levels. Psychological reactions, for example, that high-trait-anxious people might experience include worries, thoughts of doom and reduced self-confidence. Physiological reactions might include increased heart rate, respiration frequency and sweating. Behavioural reactions might include changes in usual talking levels, increased fidgeting and frequent pacing. One behavioural reaction is athletes' actual performance.

Stage 4 involves the consequences and objectively these are often dichotomous: athletes win or lose, perform above or below expectations. Understanding athletes' expectations is one factor that can help predict their interpretations of their performances and subsequent consequences. Swimmers at the Olympic Games, for example, may not win a medal or even get past the preliminary rounds in their events, but still take great pride in their achievements because they have lived up to their expected performance and attained a new personal best. Equally, some swimmers may win a silver or bronze medal, but feel they have not been successful because they believed they were good enough to win a gold one.

THE COMPETITION–PERFORMANCE RELATIONSHIP

The polarised views people hold regarding the role of competition in sport parallels similar perceptions that pervade society across numerous domains. People compete with others in all aspects of life; examples include finding romantic partners, gaining entry into education programmes, securing employment and winning sporting contests. Perhaps as a result of how widespread competition is in society, scholars from various fields (psychology, sociology, education, philosophy, etc.) have conducted considerable research examining its determinants and consequences, including the effect it has on performance in various domains. Sport psychologists have been counted among these investigators by exploring the effect competition has on athletes' performances. Divided opinion has existed across scholars regarding whether competition enhances or hinders performance.

Work by Murayama and Elliot (2012) provides an answer to the question that may appease both the proponents and opponents of competition. They argued that competition could be examined in three ways: as a characteristic of the person; the perceived situation; or the actual environment. Trait competitiveness represents a person's tendency to compete against others in an activity. For example, some people try to compete even in situations that other individuals do not consider competitive, such as the runner who treats an informal training run as a chance to beat a friend and always has to be a few steps ahead. Perceived situational competitiveness represents the degree to which a person interprets an event as involving competition. An actual competitive situation is one in which competition is built into the structure of the activity, such as sport. In light of Martens' model presented above, the actual competitive situation equates to the objective competitive situation. The perceived competitive situation equates to the subjective competitive situation. Trait competitiveness equates to a personal characteristic that influences how athletes interpret the objective situation.

Murayama and Elliot reviewed all the research they could find from any domain in life to examine if competition was related to performance. Their meta-analysis (see the Introduction to the book) indicated that there was no discernible, or at best, an extremely weak relationship between performance and both the perceived and actual competitive situation. The relationship between performance and trait competitiveness was so small as to be trivial. These results were consistent across life domains including education, work and sport.

These findings indicate that competition has no direct relationship with performance, but left open the possibility of an indirect relationship. Murayama and Elliot tested their hypothesis that competition was related to achievement goals, which in turn influenced performance, as illustrated in Figure 5.2. The two achievement goals proposed included performance approach goals and performance avoidance goals. Performance approach goals reflect people's desires to do well relative to others (similar to ego goals defined in Chapter 2 on motivation). Athletes with a performance approach goal want to show they are better at the sport than the other competitors. Performance avoidance goals represent a desire to avoid doing poorly compared with others. Athletes with a performance avoidance goal want to ensure they do not appear worse at the sport compared with others. People with an approach mind-set play to win, whereas those with an avoidance perspective do not want to lose. Athletes do not have focus on just one type of goal, but may be motivated by each to a greater or lesser extent.

According to Murayama and Elliot, competition stimulates social comparison among participants and brings normative standards of evaluation to the forefront of people's thinking. In many sports, for example, direct competition takes place where athletes are being evaluated, through the scoring system, in terms of how well they perform against each other. These social comparison processes are inherent in competition, and trigger people to adopt performance approach goals, performance avoidance goals or a mixture of both. These goals have been shown to be related with cognitions, emotions, behaviour and performance. Performance approach goals, for example, are related to eagerness, task absorption, persistence and positive performance outcomes. Performance avoidance goals are related to worry, task distraction, self-handicapping and negative performance outcomes. Murayama and Elliot conducted a second meta-analysis and three additional studies with university students to obtain support for their claim that competition has an indirect relationship with task performance (as illustrated in Figure 5.2).

Murayama and Elliot's work provides one answer to the question 'is competitive sport good or bad?' The answer is that competition is neither good nor bad, but instead it is the way that people in the situation manage the social comparison processes

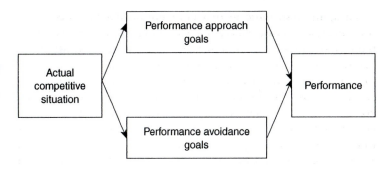

Figure 5.2: Murayama and Elliot's competition–performance relationship.

involved which influence the consequences. If the people in the situation create a social environment in which athletes become focused on avoidance goals, then they may experience anxieties and reduced performance, especially if they doubt their ability to cope with the demands. In contrast, if the leaders create an environment where athletes adopt approach goals, then performance may be enhanced. One role of coaching or leading a team is to create the environment in which players can perform optimally. Coaches and leaders who get to know athletes as individuals, and learn things such as the athletes' motives for playing, how they respond to different types of feedback and what stresses them, will have knowledge to structure the environment to help players adopt approach rather than avoidance goals.

CAN SPORT BUILD LIFE SKILLS?

A second answer to the question 'is competition good or bad?' revolves around the influence sport has on the person. Competitive sport is valued for its supposed ability to build moral character. For example, the International Olympic Committee states that

> the goal of the Olympic Movement is to contribute to building a peaceful and better world by educating youth through sport practiced without discrimination of any kind and in the Olympic spirit, which requires mutual understanding with a spirit of friendship, solidarity and fair play.
>
> (http://www.olympic.org)

The implication is that sport provides a context through which people can learn to be model citizens. At the same time, however, there are frequent examples in the media of athletes who do not appear to be acting as model and productive citizens: they get caught taking performance-enhancing drugs and cheating; they are apprehended for various crimes, including violence, theft, rape and gambling; and they abuse recreational drugs and alcohol. It is understandable that some people view claims that sport builds character with a healthy dose of scepticism.

One result of the belief that sport can be a vehicle for personal and moral growth is the development of programmes designed to build life skills. The World Health Organization (WHO) describes life skills as cognitive, emotional, interpersonal and social abilities that allow individuals to deal effectively with the challenges and demands of everyday life. The WHO (1997) has identified various life skills such as:

- *Self-awareness*: self-esteem and confidence-building, self-monitoring, self-evaluation, goal-setting, etc.
- *Self-management*: anger and stress management, time management, coping skills, controlling impulses, relaxation, etc.
- *Social awareness*: empathy, active listening, recognising and appreciating individual and group differences, etc.
- *Relationships*: negotiation, conflict management, resisting peer pressure, networking, motivation, etc.
- *Responsible decision-making*: information-gathering, critical thinking, evaluating consequences of actions, etc.

One of the reasons why sport can be a context in which children and athletes develop life skills is because these abilities are transferable. The skills described above help people cope with the demands and challenges across various domains including sport, work, education, etc. They are not unique to one domain. Also, sport is an attractive activity that many individuals enjoy. The fact that these people are open to developing abilities that will allow them to enjoy their sports provides opportunities to help them develop life skills. Nevertheless, research has indicated that these skills are not inherently or automatically learned as a result of playing sport. People can learn maladaptive and antisocial behaviours through sport as well as adaptive and prosocial actions. Character is taught, not caught. If people leading competitive sport programmes want participants to develop life skills then they need to deliberately implement strategies to that end. Life skills development occurs if coaches, sports administrators and other leaders create the right environment and learning activities (Conley *et al.* 2010).

There are numerous life skills programmes available. One example is the Sports United to Promote Education and Recreation (SUPER) programme from the Life Skills Centre,[1] located at Virginia Commonwealth University in Canada. SUPER consists of 18 workshops that address topics such as team-building, goal-setting, seeking social support, positive self-talk, identifying and developing personal strengths, etc. Programme attendees engage in three sets of activities: (a) learning physical sport specific skills; (b) developing life skills; and (c) playing the sport. Staff at the Life Skills Centre train high-school or college-student athletes to act as peer leaders and teach younger participants.

Similar to many life skills programmes, the SUPER programme is tailored to high-school and college athletes. Life skills and personal development programmes are also designed for elite athletes. Sport at the top level typically necessitates a full-time commitment, and athletes may not have sufficient opportunities to prepare themselves for life after their retirement. Many athletes finish their competitive careers in their late 20s or early 30s, and research has revealed that many may have trouble adjusting to non-sport-dominated lifestyles. To assist retiring athletes, some sporting bodies and governments have developed career assistance programmes to help them prepare for their termination from competitive elite sport. One example is the Australian Career Assistance and Education programme funded by the Australian Sports Commission and delivered through the Australian central and state institutes of sport.[2] The programme assists elite athletes to achieve sport and life goals through integrating learning, work and sports performance. To be eligible, athletes must be involved in a national senior squad or be on a scholarship with the Australian Institute of Sport or a state institute or academy of sport. Programme advisers are employed to work with athletes and their services include: career counselling and planning;

developing tailored personal development programs; educational guidance; assisting with employment preparation; providing transitional or retirement support; and making referrals to other professionals and opportunities when suitable. The programme is also delivered online. The Australian Institute of Sport[3] provides stories of how some of the more than 20,000 athletes who have participated in the programme have benefited.

A second answer to the question 'is competitive sport good or bad?' focuses on the environment that the leaders create. Sport can be an excellent context in which people develop abilities that will help them in other areas of life. Such learning, however, is not automatic, and leaders valuing such objectives need to deliberately structure the environment to allow athletes to develop these skills. Also, participants have to be aware that they have them and be confident that they can use them. Without self-efficacy and self-awareness, leaders' attempts to build life skills may not come to fruition.

HOME FIELD ADVANTAGE

One component of the objective competitive situation is the location or venue where the event is happening. There is a belief among athletes, coaches and teams that there is 'no place like home'. They believe they are more likely to win at home than when playing away. The home advantage may be defined as a performance advantage that athletes, teams or countries have when they compete at their home grounds compared with when they play at an away location under similar conditions. Researchers have accumulated evidence that the home advantage exists across sports. A meta-analysis by Jamieson (2010) of both existing research and available archival records of various sports found that the home team could be expected to win approximately 60 per cent of events. The advantage was the same for both team and individual sports and across two levels: collegiate and professional.

The home advantage was shown to have been stronger before 1950 compared with after, and three reasons might help account for the observation. (1) As sport competitions have changed and evolved there may have been changes to rules and venues that

increase the standardisation of the events. Increased standardisation reduces the home team's opportunities to take advantage of
environmental conditions, such as playing on a smaller or larger
field than normal. (2) As sport has become more commercialised,
many stadiums have become larger and may include retractable
roofs, reducing the home team's ability to take advantage of local
weather conditions. (3) Shortened travel times may be another
possible explanation for the time period effect. Although jet
lag, for example, may influence away-team performance across
national boundaries, within time zones shortened travel times
resulting from faster trains and increased air travel may lead to
fewer disruptions for athletes.

Some researchers have mooted a home field disadvantage
whereby teams playing at their own locations are proposed to
choke more often in high-pressure or championship games
compared with less critical, regular season games. Conflicting
results have emerged across individual studies. The meta-analysis
discussed above found that the home field advantage becomes
stronger from regular to championship games (rising from 59 to
63 per cent). These results indicate that although home teams do
lose and can choke in championship games, on average they are
likely to do better than during the regular season.

The meta-analysis also investigated if the home field advantage differed across specific sports. The advantage was stronger
in soccer compared with the other sports. In contrast, baseball
exhibited the weakest home field effect. Further examination
indicated that the differences among the sports may be mediated
by season length: typically, the sports with the longest seasons
were also those with the weaker home field advantage. The season
length cannot, however, provide a complete explanation because
American football, which has a short season also had one of the
weakest home advantages.

Despite these differences in terms of time period, sport and
season length, the conclusion from the meta-analysis is that home
teams have a better chance of winning than away teams. To help
explain why the phenomenon might exist, Carron and colleagues
(2005) identified specific factors that may lead to the advantage
such as a supportive crowd, venue familiarity, travel arrangements
and competition rules that favour home teams. These factors

influence athletes' psychological states. Altered psychological states lead to changes in behaviour which influence performance outcomes. For example, a supportive crowd or venue familiarity may lift the home team's confidence or motivation. In reviewing the research, however, Carron and colleagues indicated that the evidence for each of their factors was not conclusive and much remained to be learned about the specific factors involved and how they influence the phenomenon. Although clear answers may not have been forthcoming, the audience or crowd is one factor consistently proposed as having an effect. I now turn to examining the effect that crowds and audiences may have on athletes' performances.

AUDIENCE EFFECTS

Athletes typically perform in front of audiences. Events such as the Olympics and the football and rugby world cups attract a global TV audience in the billions and typically have more than one million spectators who attend the specific games and contests. Not all sporting competitions generate such interest, but even when there are no spectators, athletes are typically still observed by others, such as opponents, coaches, teammates and support staff. Researchers interested in audience effects examine how individuals perform when doing so in front of other people.

In a study, published in 1898 and often considered the first sport-psychology-related investigation, Triplett reported trends he observed when reading the archives of the Racing Board of the League of American Wheelmen. These data included the times of the following types of races: actual race times against other competitors, either paced or timed; paced races against time; and unpaced races. Triplett noted that cyclists with a pace-maker were five seconds faster than without. He hypothesised that the difference was due to the presence of other people. Triplett then designed an experiment in which children were instructed to wind a thread on a fishing reel as quickly as possible, either with another child doing the same thing, or alone. He found that children spun the reel faster when in competition with other participants than when alone. These results demonstrated the co-action effect: a phenomenon whereby enhanced performance comes about by the presence of others simultaneously and independently engaging in the same activity.

Triplett's work stimulated a line of research on social facilitation in which investigators examined the extent to which an individual's behaviour (e.g. an athlete's performance) was influenced by other people's real, imagined, or implied presence. Strictly speaking, Triplett examined the co-acting effect, because the other people involved in the situation were performing the same task as the individual being tested. Any differences may not have been due to other people merely being present, but could have resulted from the other people performing the same task. Many of the early studies that followed Triplett's work also examined the effect of co-actors on an individual's performance. From the 1960s, social facilitation research focused on whether, how and why people change their behaviour when others are just present and do not engage in the same task. The general approach has been to compare performance between at least two conditions: when the person is alone and when they are being observed.

HOW MIGHT SOCIAL FACILITATION BE EXPLAINED?

A number of explanations for social facilitation are based on arousal and stem from Zajonc's (1965) argument that the presence of others increases a performer's drive or activation levels. Increased arousal increases the probability that a person will respond to a stimulus with their dominant or most well-learned response. In tasks where the dominant response is the correct one then performance will be enhanced. In tasks where the dominant response is incorrect then performance will be impaired. In sport, for example, performance will increase for skilled athletes or in simple tasks when moving from being along to being observed by others. Performance will be hindered for novice athletes or in complex tasks.

Zajonc proposed his model in 1965, and since then researchers have suggested modifications. The evaluation–apprehension theory, for example, proposed that individuals learn that social rewards and punishments are based on other people's evaluations of them. It is the knowledge that other people are evaluating performance that influences arousal. Performance will be enhanced or impaired only in the presence of others who can approve or disapprove of a person's behaviour.

Alternative explanations have also been proposed based on other variables including attention and motivation. According to the distraction–conflict hypothesis, for example, the presence of others distracts performers and their attention is not on the task completely. There is also an increase in activation. Performance will drop on complex tasks, whereas on simple tasks it will increase or decrease depending on the extent to which activation has increased. Most of the social facilitation research in sport has focused on the arousal-based explanations rather than the other explanations.

In 1983, Bond and Titus published a large meta-analysis examining the social facilitation research generally. Across 241 studies that had used just under 24,000 participants, the authors concluded that the presence of others: (a) increases the speed of simple task performance and decreases the speed of complex task performance; (b) impairs complex performance accuracy and slightly facilitates simple task performance accuracy; (c) is unrelated to performers' evaluation apprehension; and (d) heightens individuals' physiological arousal only if they are performing complex tasks. Overall these effects were small indicating that social facilitation did not have a large influence on performance, and did not fully support the arousal-based explanations.

When considering the influence of social facilitation on movement or sport-related skills, it may be useful to consider the types of abilities being examined (Strauss 2002). Broadly, three types of movement abilities can be considered including: (a) conditioning-based abilities, or those that place large demands on the energy systems, such as running or weightlifting; (b) coordination-based abilities, or those that place demands on the synchronisation of body systems, such as golf or shooting; and (c) tasks that involve equal measures of both conditioning and coordination, such as many team sports (e.g. soccer, hockey, netball). There are conflicting results regarding the effect of social facilitation on coordination-based or mixed (coordination and conditioning) task performance. Output on power or stamina-based tasks (i.e. conditioning-based tasks) seem to be enhanced, although the effect is small. Overall, if there are relationships between social facilitation and movement or sport-based tasks, these effects are generally weak.

Although social facilitation theory and research has focused a great deal on the type of task being examined, it could also be that differences among athletes may influence the effect on performance (Uziel 2007). Social orientation is one individual difference that seems to have support. There are two broad social orientations. The first is a positive orientation that involves a tendency towards self-assurance and enthusiasm in general and the social environment, and is reflected in high extraversion and self-esteem. The second is a negative orientation that involves a tendency toward anxiety and apprehension in general and toward the social environment, and is reflected in high neuroticism and low self-esteem. It seems that both orientations moderate the social facilitation and performance relationship. The positive orientation is associated with a performance benefit, whereas the negative disposition is debilitating. In individuals who adopt a positive orientation, the presence of others is associated with increased performance. In those adopting a negative orientation, there is a performance decrement. These effects are independent of the type of task, either simple or complex.

The topic of social facilitation illustrates that sport psychology knowledge is only as good as the quality of the underpinning research. When studying social facilitation, researchers compare people's performance when they are alone (the 'alone condition') with when others are present (the 'presence of others condition'). An important issue has been the question of what constitutes an adequate alone condition. Often the alone condition has been contaminated by the researchers' presence, so the participants have not really been on their own when performing the task (the scientist has still been in the room). When accounting for the two types of conditions, the effect of other people's presence (in the presence of others condition) is stronger when compared with 'true' performing alone conditions than when contaminated alone conditions are used. When related to the social orientation research, the performance enhancement effect for the positive social orientation and the decrement for the negative disposition are stronger when a true alone condition is the comparison than when scientists are present. Without knowing this flaw in research design, sport psychologists might reach inaccurate conclusions.

SUMMARY

Earlier in the chapter I highlighted how the role of competition in sport and other domains generates polarised views regarding its value, often based on personal experience and anecdotes. Situations similar to the one at the start of the chapter have occurred in many schools. Coach Reynolds' observations can be understood through the lens of the information presented above. Competition is inherent in the structure of sport and the activity stimulates social comparison processes. People who have coached will typically testify that even when not keeping score, such as in warm-up games in team sports, players are often still comparing each other in some way based around their competence in the activity. The social comparison that occurs is not either good or bad, but can have positive and negative consequences. Similar to most endeavours, the way that the human interactions and communications are managed have a significant bearing on the type of consequences that result. Although Jayne above might believe that competition helped him achieve in business, it is likely that he developed and was shown skills to manage the process and how to transfer these abilities to the commercial domain. Zoe and Hoban are also partially correct in saying that there can be negative psychological and behavioural consequences. These results likely occur when people do not learn how: to interpret winning and losing in adaptive ways, to evaluate their competence in a variety of criteria and to separate their self-worth from a sporting activity. In many sporting contexts positive consequences can occur if the leaders involved in the activity develop an atmosphere that focuses on striving for personal achievement, as much as one that focuses on meeting the competitive demands of the situation.

NOTES

1 http://www.lifeskills.vcu.edu/index.html.
2 http://www.ausport.gov.au/ais/athlete_career_and_education.
3 http://www.ausport.gov.au/ais/athlete_career_and_education/resources.

REFERENCES

Bond, C. F. and Titus, L. J. (1983). Social facilitation: A meta-analysis of 241 studies. *Psychological Bulletin, 94*, 265–292.

Carron, A. V., Loughhead, T. M. and Bray, S. R. (2005). The home advantage in sport competitions: Courneya and Carron's (1992) conceptual framework a decade later. *Journal of Sports Sciences, 23*, 395–407.

Conley, K. A., Danish, S. J. and Pasquariello, C. D. (2010). Sport as a context for teaching life skills. In S. J. Hanrahan and M. B. Andersen (Eds), *Routledge handbook of applied sport psychology* (pp. 168–176). London: Routledge.

Jamieson, J. P. (2010). The home field advantage in athletics: A meta-analysis. *Journal of Applied Social Psychology, 40*, 1819–1848.

Martens, R. M. (1975). *Social psychology and physical activity*. New York: Harper & Row.

Murayama, K. and Elliot, A. J. (2012). The competition–performance relation: A meta-analytic review and test of the opposing processes model of competition and performance. *Psychological Bulletin, 138*, 1035–1070.

Strauss, B. (2002). Social facilitation in motor tasks: A review of research and theory. *Psychology of Sport and Exercise, 3*, 237–256.

Uziel, L. (2007). Individual differences in the social facilitation effect: A review and meta-analysis. *Journal of Research in Personality, 41*, 579–601.

World Health Organization (1997). *Life skills education for children and adolescents in schools*. Geneva: Author.

Zajonc, R. B. (1965). Social facilitation. *Science, 149*, 269–274.

GROUP PROCESSES

CHAPTER LEARNING OBJECTIVES

1 Define a group and detail how groups develop.
2 Examine the relationship between group size and productivity.
3 Define cohesion.
4 Detail the relationship between cohesion and sports performance.
5 Explore cohesion correlates.
6 Describe leadership effectiveness and the coach–athlete relationship.
7 Detail common team-building interventions.

Liam is the popular and well-respected player/coach of the Hyperion Angels, a mixed touch rugby team sponsored by the Hyperion Hotel. The players have given him the nickname 'Angelus' because he is the Angels' leader. The team formed in 1999 and since then have won the league several times. In the past few seasons, their main rivals have been The Wolves, sponsored by the law firm Wolfram & Hart and led by one of Liam's work colleagues, Lindsey McDonald. This year the Angels have been struggling and performing poorly, partly due to recent player turnover. Among their losses was Cordelia, one of the long-standing and talented female players. Cordelia was replaced with Faith, a young player with a fiery temper. The team has always had a good reputation for player conduct, but in the previous three games Faith had been frequently penalised for foul language and unsporting behaviour. As the season has progressed infighting has emerged among some of the players, particularly Wesley and Charles. One night, for example, Charles accused Wesley of not being committed to the team and Liam had to separate the two players. Liam thinks that the team's lack of unity has been contributing to their poor performances and has been unsure what he can do to change the situation. When talking about it one morning at work, Lindsey told him to throw the team a barbecue and supply them with alcohol.

Liam's perception that the lack of unity is contributing to the Angels' poor performance echoes a popular belief within sport and society generally. People often work in groups to achieve goals in various domains including sport, the military, education, science, the arts and business, and they consistently believe that close-knit teams are more successful than those characterised by discord. Frequently in sport, coaches and players will attribute success and failure to the high level or lack of team cohesion. Although people recognise readily that group dynamics are integral to successful sport teams, such interactions also typically contribute to the training and performance of athletes in individuals sports. These athletes often belong to squads and train or compete in group settings.

The responsibility for managing team unity typically falls to coaches, managers, captains and other people in leadership positions. Leaders are usually interested in knowing how they can manage and direct group processes and dynamics to ensure successful team performance. To assist coaches and team mangers, sport psychologists have studied group dynamics and leadership extensively. In this chapter I will (a) define a group and detail how groups develop; (b) examine the relationship between group size and productivity; (c) examine team cohesion, its correlates and its relationship with performance; (d) describe leadership effectiveness and the coach–athlete relationship; and (e) detail common team-building interventions.

DEFINING A GROUP

What makes a number of individuals a 'group' or a 'team'? It is an interesting classroom activity to ask sport psychology students to define a group, or to ask some sport spectators having a drink in a pub the same question, because the discussion can be engaging. Many individuals suggest that a group involves two or more people who interact with each other and who work towards a common goal. Other characteristics of groups and teams emerging from the discussions may include shared values or norms and the presence of team roles. These views help explain why sports teams are groups. There is typically a common goal, individuals define themselves as group members, and there are often structured and defined roles.

Smaller groups may also exist within larger ones. At the Olympics, for example, within the national squad, there may be sport specific teams, such as those for archery, swimming or cycling. During their sporting events, however, members of these teams typically compete as individuals.

In sport, teams can be categorised according to the interactions members have with each other, including:

- *Independent teams:* Individuals compete separately (e.g. gymnasts).
- *Reactive teams:* Individuals respond to their teammates' actions, but not always at the same time (e.g. the softball catcher, pitcher, fielder and person holding base).
- *Coactive teams:* Individuals compete side by side with limited interaction (e.g. canoeists).
- *Interactive teams:* Individuals continuously interact with each other throughout the contest (e.g. soccer, volleyball).

Understanding the various ways athletes from different sports interact with each other helps people appreciate how group dynamics and team processes may need to be tailored to ensure optimal functioning.

A question that has interested researchers has been: how does a collection of individuals come together to be a productive group? A widely cited framework detailing group development or lifecycle goes by the phrase: forming, storming, norming, performing and adjourning (Tuckman and Jensen, 1977).

- When *forming*, individuals familiarise themselves which each other and establish the group's purpose.
- *Storming* occurs due to conflicts that arise (e.g. disagreements regarding group goals).
- During *norming* conflict is resolved, cohesion increases and group norms and standards of behaviour arise.
- *Performing* takes place when the group is operating effectively in pursuit of its goals.
- *Adjourning* ensues following task completion and reduced contact among members.

The model above adopts a linear approach to group development. Many athletes and coaches in sport realise that teams do not always proceed in such a manner. For example, teams may experience storming when they are performing. Group development may be better described as consisting of repeated cycles. One such approach includes the following stages (Arrow *et al.*, 2004):

1 *Discontent*: Athletes do not identify with and feel alienated from the team (e.g. new players or those having difficulties with coaches).
2 *Group identification*: Players may be retained or dropped through the selection process and there is increased commitment among the team's selected athletes.
3 *Group productivity*: Athletes focus on production and contributing to the team.
4 *Individuation*: Members start to demand recognition for their contributions (e.g. athletes may become dissatisfied with their roles and seek change).
5 *Decay*: Players become less interested in being group members, leading to a return to the discontent stage, group change or abandonment.

One key point in both approaches is that conflict and disagreement is a normal part of a team's lifecycle. Rather than viewing conflict as an issue to be avoided, it may serve team-functioning better to accept that disagreements are likely to occur and that finding ways to manage such encounters may yield benefits for group-functioning. For example, the disagreement between Charles and Wesley above may reflect that both players are committed to the team, but they express it differently, and once they both realise this fact they might learn ways to assist each other to maximise their potential.

Group dynamics is a topic with a voluminous body of literature, perhaps reflecting the value ascribed to it in daily life. It is beyond the scope of the current chapter to do the topic justice, and instead I have selected aspects from the literature to provide a flavour of the work sport psychologists have conducted. One topic that has interested psychologists and athletes alike has been group size and productivity to which I now turn.

GROUP SIZE AND PRODUCTIVITY

The study of the effect of group size on team and individual productivity can be traced back to work undertaken by a French agricultural engineer, Max Ringelmann, in the 1880s and published in 1913 when he examined factors influencing maximum performance when workers were pushing or pulling a load horizontally. He found that as group size increased, there was a tendency for individual members to become increasingly less productive. This observation became known as the Ringelmann effect. He identified motivation and coordination losses as two possible reasons for the effect. He favoured coordination losses, suggesting the workers were increasingly unable to synchronise their efforts.

The following equation provides a useful framework for understanding group productivity:

$$Actual\ Productivity = Potential\ Productivity - Motivation\ and\ Coordination\ Losses$$

As the number of people in a group increases, potential productivity increases because the pool of human resources, skills and capabilities expands. Nevertheless, at some point additional people will not increase potential productivity because the necessary resources to achieve the task will be available. At the same time, however, with increasing group size it becomes more difficult to run the team efficiently (coordination losses), and players may become less keen to supply an optimal effort (motivation losses). For example, coaches may not be able to give as much individual instruction to each player as desired, and some athletes may be less inclined to interact with all the other team members. Although team productivity may increase, so do process and motivation losses, and the relative contribution per player decreases. In the Hyperion Angels above, although a minimum of seven players is needed to field a team, increasing the number may lead to improved performance, because players can be substituted throughout a game so they remain fresh and avoid fatigue. There comes a point, however, where additional players will not increase performance, because there are already enough to ensure they are fresh when they enter the fray. Above this number, team performance might start to decrease because there are too many players to coordinate effectively and some individuals may lose interest in the game or become upset, because they are not getting sufficient game time.

Although Ringelmann, and other researchers following in his footsteps, believed that the effect was probably due to coordination rather than motivation losses, later investigations revealed that the relative decrease in individual performance was primarily due to a loss of motivation. The possibility that motivation losses account for the Ringelmann effect may be explained by social loafing.

Social loafing occurs when people exert less effort when working in teams than when working alone (Karau and Williams, 1993). Tug-of-war provides the classic often-used example. As group size increases, the amount of effort each person provides decreases. Identifying when social loafing occurs and ways to reduce it has occupied psychologists' minds since Ringelmann published his work and the knowledge has implications for sporting leaders.

The risk of social loafing increases when athletes' productivity cannot be evaluated independently or they think their efforts are redundant and not unique. Whereas traditionally in some team sports social loafing might have occurred because it was difficult to assess a person's performance, the increase in video analysis has provided ways for coaching staff to obtain objective indices of each individual's effort. In rugby union, for example, with video analysis it is possible to obtain a large number of statistics for each player, including the number of tackles made or broken successfully, metres gained per run with the ball, or minutes in a game spent walking, running or jogging. In addition, the video analysis allows coaches to focus on one particular aspect, such as sitting down with the player and reviewing every attempted tackle to help identify ways to improve technique. Sports leaders and coaches who identify ways to assess the contributions of individual players may find that social loafing reduces in their squads.

Players may also loaf when they perceive the task to be meaningless and when they have no personal involvement in its achievement, such as when players do not think their efforts will have an influence on a game or the result is a foregone conclusion. One challenge for a leader is to help players realise how their roles contribute to the achievement of a meaningful team goal. Helping players believe in the value of the group's goals and that they are making a valued contribution will likely reduce social loafing.

Social loafing may also ensue when it is difficult to evaluate the team's performance against suitable criteria. Many times in sport, the opposition provide a standard by which to evaluate the team's performance. In situations where the difference between the opposing athletes or teams is large enough to reduce any uncertainty regarding the performance, teams may develop a new goal such as scoring a specific number of points or not allowing the opposition to achieve certain objectives. For example, at half time a hockey team being beaten by superior opponents may treat the second half as a new game and attempt to 'win' it by scoring more points.

Evidence reveals that social loafing may emerge when other people in the squad are strangers or are expected to perform well. Helping athletes to realise that team success is dependent on the contributions each person makes, and an outstanding performance by a single individual will likely be insufficient to help the squad achieve its goal may help reduce social loafing. Increasing team cohesion may also minimise the phenomenon, and is the focus of the next section.

TEAM COHESION

Similar to the definition of a group above, students and spectators can have lively discussions about what team cohesion represents. Some individuals refer to classic definitions of cohesion when they suggest that it includes the sum of the forces that keep individuals in an interacting group. Other people focus on how attracted members are to the group, how well the collective individuals can withstand external disruption, or the similarity of people's beliefs, opinions, needs and goals. Each of these viewpoints helps define essential elements in cohesion. Sport psychologists commonly suggest that group cohesion is the propensity of a sports team to stay together in the striving for their objectives and athlete satisfaction. This definition highlights that both goal achievement and member satisfaction are the desired outcomes of a team.

Under the group cohesion label, sport psychologists often differentiate between social and task cohesion. Social cohesion refers to the extent athletes get on with each other and find their teammates enjoyable company. Task cohesion represents the extent athletes in a team work together to achieve their common goals.

Team cohesion is multidimensional rather than being a simple unitary idea. Part of the multidimensional aspect arises from players having multiple perceptions regarding the group as an entity and its attractiveness to them. Two perceptions psychologists typically examine include:

1 *Group integration*: Perceptions regarding group closeness and unification.
2 *Individual attraction*: Athletes' perceptions regarding their motivations to be part of the group and their personal feelings about the team.

These two perceptions can be viewed from two foci:

1 *Task orientation*: Inclination towards striving to achieve the team's goals.
2 *Social orientation*: Desire to develop and maintain social relationships in the team.

These two foci and two perceptions combine to yield four dimensions to cohesion (Carron *et al.*, 1985): integration–task, integration–social, attraction–task and attraction–social. These four dimensions can provide a framework to help psychologists and coaches assess the needs of a team.

As a further dimension, cohesion is instrumental. Sports teams typically do not stay united for the purpose of staying together. They typically remain united for a task-related purpose. For example, although players may join a social sports team to gain enjoyment, the group still has a task-basis to their existence (even a social football team plays games).

THE COHESION–PERFORMANCE RELATIONSHIP

Cohesion is highly prized among athletes and coaches because they believe that it influences performance. There are, however, examples of teams that have performed well but have not been cohesive. Similarly, many cohesive teams have failed to achieve their sporting goals. Sport psychologists have expended considerable effort in examining the relationship cohesion has with sports performance. Carron and colleagues' meta-analysis (2002) provides some evidence for athletes' and coaches' beliefs. They synthesised 46 studies involving about 10,000 athletes and over 1,000 teams. There was a moderate to large relationship between cohesion and performance. The relationship was observed in both directions: increases in both task and social cohesion contributed to enhanced performance. Increases in performance, in turn, contributed to enhanced social and task cohesion.

In addition to identifying a relationship between cohesion and performance, Carron and colleagues examined possible moderators of the relationship. A moderator is a variable that influences a relationship between two factors. Gender, for example, was one variable that adjusted the relationship between cohesion and performance. Carron and colleagues observed that the relationship was stronger in female teams compared with male squads (although there was still a significant association for men). Apart from gender, no other variable acted as a moderator. The relationship between cohesion and performance did not vary with type of sport (coactive or interactive), performance measure (self-reported or behavioural) or level of athlete. The type of cohesion measure also did not influence the result (e.g. task, social or generic). These findings justify attempts to develop sports team cohesion as a way to increase performance. Possible ways to develop cohesion will be explored below.

COHESION CORRELATES

As well as performance, sport psychologists have also searched for other factors associated with cohesion. Understanding factors that are correlated with cohesion may yield implications for athletes, coaches and teams. Knowing about the contributors and barriers to cohesion, for example, may help teams to structure their organisations to maximise group togetherness. Also, identifying the benefits of cohesion, beyond performance, might help some teams decide how much value they should place on building player unity and camaraderie relative to the other demands involved in their sport. Increased knowledge might also help people to identify ways to develop cohesion so they can reap performance and other benefits. The majority of the research, however, has been descriptive, and as discussed in the Introduction to the book, such work does not allow causal relationships to be established. Despite this limitation with much of the research, it is likely that the relationships are bidirectional and the variables influence each other (Carron *et al.* 2007).

ENVIRONMENTAL FACTORS

Two factors commonly identified under the environmental label include team size and level of competition (Carron *et al.*, 2007). Broadly, as the size of a team increases, there is a decrease in cohesion. Possibly, as the size increases it becomes difficult to communicate and coordinate team activities. Also player motivation may be reduced. In a similar way, cohesion decreases with increased level of competition. Perhaps cohesion is higher in lower-level teams because with less experienced players it is easier to reach consensus regarding team goals.

ATHLETE FACTORS

Three widely cited athlete factors correlated with cohesion include similarity, satisfaction and adherence (Carron *et al.*, 2007). First, cohesion is higher in groups of athletes who are similar to each other, across a range of demographic and individual differences, compared with teams where the personnel are dissimilar. It may be that people who are similar find it easier to communicate and interact. Second, there is evidence that satisfaction is related with cohesion and performance in a circular fashion. Cohesion enhances satisfaction which leads to good performance (happy athletes like to train with each other). Then increased success builds satisfaction which leads to cohesion (happy athletes feel closer to their teammates). Third, cohesion correlates with adherence, probably because perceptions of cohesion are related with attending training and competition, being on time and perceptions of resilience.

TEAM FACTORS

Team factors include norms, roles and collective efficacy (Carron and Eys, 2012). First, increased cohesion is associated with conformity to group norms and the relationship may, or may not, benefit the team. If the team norms focus on striving for excellence, for example, the conformity to norms may benefit the team through enhanced performance or as a way to ensure recruits are productive. Second, evidence indicates cohesion is related with role clarity, acceptance and performance. If the relationships are bidirectional then increasing cohesion may help players settle into their roles. Also, ensuring players know what their contributions and roles in a team are may increase cohesion. Third, collective efficacy shares a similar relationship with cohesion and performance as athlete satisfaction. Collective efficacy is a group's shared belief in its combined resources to undertake actions to achieve a task. Enhancing either cohesion or performance increases collective efficacy which then improves the other variable.

LEADERSHIP FACTORS

Leaders can have an influential role on athletes' perceptions of cohesion. High levels of task cohesion, for example, are associated with leadership behaviours involving a focus on instruction, skill development, training and positive feedback. Also, high cohesion is associated with a democratic decision-making style. Such a style refers to the degree that leaders allow or encourage athletes to share or participate in team decision-making processes. Given the role that leaders play in team cohesion and in sport more generally, it has been a popular topic of study among psychologists, and is examined in the next section.

LEADERSHIP

A leader is an individual who influences another person or group of people towards achieving a common goal. In sport, some people hold a formal or prescribed leadership position, such as coach, captain or manager. Other people might occupy an informal position that has not been prescribed, but they still hold sway over the group. In managing the group dynamics, leaders operate at both the team and individual levels. Leadership involves both behavioural and achievement-focused components because those in charge of a group are attempting to direct members' actions towards a goal (even if the goal is to have fun).

Sport psychologists have drawn on many theories to identify effective leadership characteristics. These have included theories focused on the person's personality traits or the situation factors influencing effective leadership. Models providing the best and most useful explanations focus on the interaction between leaders' characteristics and the environments in which they operate (Riemer 2007). The implication is that a person who is an effective leader in one situation may not necessarily be successful in another environment with a different group. The two theories presented in this chapter have received considerable attention from sport psychologists in recent years.

MULTIDIMENSIONAL MODEL OF LEADERSHIP

The multidimensional model of leadership is one of the most widely cited theories on the topic discussed in sport psychology. It is illustrated in Figure 6.1 (Chelladurai 2013), which presents the model in four levels: transformational leadership; the antecedents of a leader's actions; leadership behaviour; and consequences. As shown in the diagram, consequences include athlete satisfaction and team performance, and these are influenced by the congruency among the leader's actual behaviour, the athlete's preferred leadership behaviour and the required behaviour demanded of the person in the role. As the congruency among the three aspects increases, there is greater athlete satisfaction and team performance. For example, if the athletes and situation both prefer and require an autocratic approach, and the actual leadership behaviour is despotic, then there are likely to be high levels of congruency, and the prediction would be enhanced player satisfaction and optimal team performance.

Coaches' knowledge and perceptions of the athletes' and situational preferences and requirements influence their actual behaviour. A rugby union coach, for example, who knows that a team prefers an attacking style of play, that players have the necessary skills and that recent rule changes favour this approach, will likely be successful by building game tactics around such an approach. Flexibility in adjusting team tactics to changing player preferences or situation requirements will also contribute to coaching efficacy. For example, if the rugby team's performance slips during a game because their tactics do not suit the conditions or the opponent's defensive screens, then the coach may direct the players to change their style in some way.

Moving further up Figure 6.1, three types of antecedents influence actual, required and preferred leadership behaviour, and include athlete, situational and coach characteristics. Examples of athletes' characteristics may include their needs, abilities and circumstances. To illustrate, if players believe that their technical proficiency is lacking then they may prefer a leader to spend time coaching them in basic skills of the sport. Regarding situational characteristics, examples may include organisational structure, culture and the broader context. In some sporting competitions, for instance, there might be league regulations detailing that teams have to adhere to specific fair play standards, such as not showing disrespect to officials. As a result of these regulations, to be effective, coaches may have to know how to manage volatile players. Leaders' own characteristics are the third type of antecedent influence on behaviour detailed in Figure 6.1. A coach with high levels of self-awareness, for example, may have insight into her strengths and weaknesses. She will be able to draw on her reflections when selecting support staff to ensure that the necessary coaching skills are available to the players.

At the top level of the Figure 6.1, transformational leadership influences coach, athlete and situational characteristics. Transformational leadership is discussed in the next section, but according to the multidimensional model, these individuals modify situational and athlete characteristics: by altering goals, values and norms; by providing a vision; and by instilling confidence.

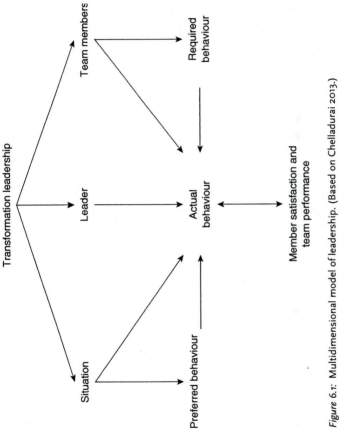

Figure 6.1: Multidimensional model of leadership. (Based on Chelladurai 2013.)

Although transformational leaders may be highly effective, it is not necessary that coaches be such inspirational people for a team to do well. Individuals who are not transformational can still be effective coaches if their behaviour fits the situation and meets the needs of the athletes involved.

TRANSFORMATIONAL LEADERSHIP

A relatively recent development has been the study of transformational leadership in sport. Some leaders, coaches and managers in sport seem to inspire athletes to reach high levels of performance and achieve beyond their expectations. Examples of such coaches might include Alex Ferguson (soccer), Phil Jackson (basketball) and Don Shula (American football). Transformational leadership theory may provide a framework that advances our understanding of why these individuals are effective (Bass and Riggio 2005). Transformational leaders are charismatic individuals who inspire followers to extraordinary outcomes. These coaches also encourage players to become leaders themselves by empowering them and aligning the team's goals with those of the members. The following four components help us to appreciate why these people can influence others so dramatically:

1   *Idealised influence.* Transformational leaders are admired, respected, trusted and act as role models. Group members identify with transformational leaders, want to emulate them, and endow them with extraordinary attributes (e.g. persistence, determination and skills). These leaders are happy to take risks, are consistent rather than arbitrary in their decision-making and behaviour and have high standards of moral conduct.
2   *Inspirational motivation.* These leaders inspire and arouse followers by providing meaningful goals and high but realistic challenges. They communicate enthusiasm, optimism and clear expectations. These people also encourage and build team spirit and identity.
3   *Intellectual stimulation.* Transformational leaders fuel group members' efforts to be creative and innovative by questioning current beliefs and procedures, reframing issues and difficulties and

viewing existing situations from new perspectives. Such leaders do not engage in public criticism, but encourage new ideas and novel problem-solving strategies from group members. Followers are included in the process of addressing problems and searching for solutions.

4 *Individualised consideration.* Leaders act as mentors and focus on individual group members' needs for growth and achievement. They provide learning opportunities within a supportive context. Tasks are delegated as a way to develop group members. Differences among group members are recognised and accepted. Reciprocal communication is encouraged and interactions are personalised.

Over the past 30 years there has been considerable research examining the correlates of transformational leadership in a variety of domains including commerce, education, health and sport. Reviewers of this research conclude that the leadership style relates positively to objective and subjective performance in these various areas, and there is some supportive evidence within the sporting context. In addition, this governance style is related to perceived and objective leadership effectiveness, followers' job satisfaction, leadership satisfaction and motivation.

Further, investigators have also attempted to identify the reasons why this leadership approach might relate with performance, and a number of possible explanations have been supported. For example, transformational leaders may enhance group members' self-efficacy or intrinsic motivation, which in turn increases persistence and performance. As a second example, these leaders inspire members to identify with them and to desire to emulate their achievements, which leads to increased effort and performance. As a third example, through aligning organisational and group members' goals and values, transformational leaders are able to focus efforts in a coordinated fashion, leading to enhanced productivity.

COACH–ATHLETE RELATIONSHIP

In many athletic settings coaches are the primary leaders and understanding their relationships with athletes likely yields benefits for people involved in sport. Coaches, for example, who know how to build good relationships with players may find athletes are more receptive to their ideas. Jowett (2007) and her colleagues in recent years have proposed that the coach–athlete relationship has four dimensions: closeness, commitment, complementarity and co-orientation. Closeness refers to the emotional bond between the parties, and includes trust, care and support. Commitment represents the desire to maintain the relationship both currently and in the future. Complementarity refers to coaches' and athletes' cooperative and affiliative interactions. Co-orientation denotes coaches' and athletes' common ground or the congruence of their perceptions regarding their relationship. The coach–athlete relationship may be described as one of the 'glues' that bind a team together. Relationships with high levels of closeness, commitment and complementarity are associated with:

- increased team cohesion;
- greater role clarity;
- motivational climates emphasising skill-learning, improvement and prosocial values;
- greater athlete and interpersonal satisfaction;
- enhanced performance.

There are several strategies and attitudes that coaches and athletes can adopt to help develop their relationships. Identifying reasons to trust, respect and appreciate the other person, treating each other consistently and fairly and being empathetic and supportive may help enhance closeness, for example. Ensuring both parties have a shared understanding of goals, their roles, values and reasons for being in the team may assist with commitment. It may also help the relationship if the people involved get to know the other individual on a personal level and adopt an open stance and share things about themselves. One advantage of getting to know each other on a personal level is that coaches and athletes then learn how to best express their trust, respect and concern for the other person. Some athletes, for example, might respond well to caring words or even a hug, whereas others may respond better to pragmatic attempts to demonstrate concern (e.g. making a person a cup of tea to create time so the individual has the opportunity to talk).

HELPING THE HYPERION ANGELS: TEAM-BUILDING INTERVENTIONS

People associated with sport often value team-building interventions as a way to achieve various goals including: increased performance and training behaviour; enhanced athlete commitment, satisfaction and enjoyment; clear team roles, goals and norms; optimising team processes; and improved interpersonal relationships. Leaders and coaches may employ a great variety of interventions, ranging from social events to team-building camps involving participation in vigorous physical activities (e.g. rock-climbing, the armed forces basic training and sailing). At the same time, athletes may view these team-building activities as lacking in value, other than allowing leaders to feel like they are competent. One reason why people may think that such interventions do not achieve anything is because these strategies are sometimes used without sufficient planning. Leaders and coaches may just assume that individuals become a team when they interact or have fun together. Without thought, however, interaction may also lead to increased conflict and mistrust. Team-building interventions can be effective if people identify what they are hoping to achieve and implement strategies to achieve these objectives. The barbecue with alcohol that Lindsey suggested to Liam above may reflect his belief that simply spending time together is enough to solve team conflict. A barbecue could be an excellent and feasible idea, but Liam might be advised, however, to think about how his group of players might react if alcohol loosens individuals' inhibitions.

PLANNING AND USING INTERVENTIONS

A straightforward approach to team-building interventions includes: (a) objective setting; (b) strategy matching and implementation; and (c) evaluation and maintenance. Group dynamics and team cohesion fluctuate over time. The initial phase in developing effective team-building interventions is to identify the reasons for expending effort and money, particularly when people may have busy lives outside of sport or there are limited resources, as is likely to be the case for the Hyperion Angels. To illustrate, Liam might review the four dimensions associated with cohesion (integration–task, integration–social, attraction–task and attraction–social) and decide which ones need the most development in his team. Such a decision would guide his planning, intervention selection, implementation and evaluation. He might, for example, focus on developing good team processes, structure, roles or norms. To achieve these aims, Liam might make use of goal-setting principles (see Chapter 7) to develop clear, specific and measurable objectives. The level of goal-setting and planning may vary depending on the team's needs and situation. Professional teams may invest more money, time and personnel than what Liam probably has at his disposal.

Having established the objectives, the next phase is to identify the strategies best suited to achieving the objectives, the athletes and the situation. Strategies do not have to be activities that are in addition to typical or normal team procedures. Instead, they can be part of the normal day-to-day life of the team, such as ensuring good communication occurs, players regularly meet and there are opportunities for players to discuss issues. With respect to the Hyperion Angels, Liam can achieve a great deal without the need for separate, unusual or expensive activities.

Nevertheless, Liam might decide that an additional strategy or event might be useful. The scientific literature is replete with strategies Liam could use to help the Angels and he might even consider asking a sport psychologist to help. Skilled practitioners are able to use the strategies presented in the literature in creative ways that suit the situation and secure buy-in from the athletes. There are many psychologists, managerial consultants and others advertising their expertise in group development. Many of these people advertise on the internet and leaders can search to identify them and learn about possible strategies. Similar to many aspects of applied sport psychology, the effectiveness of any intervention Liam tries will be influenced by the degree to which the players accept the need for them and willingly contribute to their effectiveness.

One comment that athletes in the Angels may make about team-building activities is that they do not observe lasting changes. Instead, the ideas, decisions or cohesive spirit that was generated are forgotten as the team returns to its normal activities, and as personnel and circumstances change. Identifying ways to review and maintain progress when developing objectives and strategies will help Liam to carry forward momentum bred from the initial activities.

EXAMPLE TEAM-BUILDING STRATEGIES

There are some variables that influence cohesion over which Liam may have limited control. For example, although it may be desirable to limit player turnover or team size, most probably Liam, like most coaches, will not have sufficient freedom to manage these factors. Liam, for example, may have to accept that Cordelia has left and been replaced by Faith. Example strategies that Liam may be able to implement are presented below.

- *Set group goals.* Developing team goals may help the Angels' members to develop a common understanding of their team's purpose and activities. Similar to goal-setting on an individual athlete basis, helping the Angels to develop group objectives may enhance their focus, motivation, persistence, problem-solving and identification of achievement strategies. Chapter 7 discusses goal-setting in greater detail. Although group goal-setting helps ensure players are 'singing from the same song sheet', the team may benefit from engaging in debate and critical reflection. The absence of debate might indicate the presence of the groupthink phenomenon. Groupthink reflects a type of interaction characterised by attempts to minimise conflict and obtain a consensus without testing and evaluating ideas. The group may make irrational decisions or fail to accurately understand the position in the broader context. Groupthink may occur in groups that do not have interaction with outsiders or do not have clear rules for decision-making, and where the people involved have similar backgrounds.
- *Establish role clarity and acceptance.* Team goal-setting might also contribute to enhanced role clarity and acceptance. The Angel's cohesion will probably improve when the players understand what their own and teammates' roles are within the squad and how they and others can fulfil their obligations. Some roles in the Angels are likely to be more desirable than others, such as starters versus non-starters. A challenge for Liam is to help people in each role to accept their position and appreciate the contribution they are making.
- *Formulate common norms and values.* The goal-setting process might also provide an opportunity to discuss team norms and values. Cohesion improves when players ascribe to similar

beliefs and ways of behaving. In this regard, the team may benefit from Liam helping Faith to control her fiery temper if the squad values its reputation for prosocial behaviour. Leaders who invite players to identify and police team norms, values and ground rules encourage them to take ownership and have an active part in the maintenance of a team's daily activities.

- *Communicate effectively.* Open, supportive, empathetic and clear communication helps to prevent and resolve issues and conflicts. Such communication also leads to people feeling they have been heard and are valued members of a team. One advantage of a barbecue or other social events where people relax is that team members learn about each other, including the ways they typically express themselves and communicate. Getting to know each other on a personal level may assist the quality of team communication during training and competition.
- *Develop identity and distinctiveness.* Identifying events, symbols, articles of clothing, history, etc. that promote a sense of identity and distinctiveness among the Angels may help players to feel they are part of a valued group or a sense of cohesion among the group. The use of a training or dress uniform, for example, may help them look and feel like a team. Some coaches have observed that training intensity increases when players are in similar clothes and that they behave like a team in dress uniform. As another example, drawing on a shared history, such as a cultural or community background, may also enhance identity and distinctiveness.

CONCLUSION

Sport psychology can be defined as the study of an athlete's behaviour, thinking and feelings in sport. Such a definition directs the focus to the individual level. Athletes, however, operate in a social and physical context. The study of group dynamics and processes helps psychologists consider the immediate social sport environment within which athletes perform and adds a level of complexity to the discipline. A complete examination of the basics of group dynamics would require its own textbook (e.g. Carron and Eys 2012). Instead, some of the interesting and relevant aspects have been presented in this chapter. These aspects, however, reveal that groups have a significant influence on athlete behaviour and that there is much that leaders can do at the group level to enhance performance. The next two chapters continue with the applied theme, first by examining typical methods that sport psychologists employ to help athletes with their mental skills and then strategies coaches can use to assist with physical skills and behaviours.

REFERENCES

Arrow, H., Poole, M. S., Henry, K. B., Whelan, S. and Moreland, R. (2004). Time, change, and development: The temporal perspective on groups. *Small Group Research, 35,* 73–105.

Bass, B. M. and Riggio, R. E. (2005). *Transformational leadership.* New York: Psychology Press.

Carron, A. V. and Eys, M. A. (2012). *Group dynamics in sport* (4th ed.). Morgantown, WV: Fitness Information Technology.

Carron, A. V., Widmeyer, W. N. and Browley, L. R. (1985). The development of an instrument to assess cohesion in sport: The group environment questionnaire. *Journal of Sport Psychology, 7,* 244–266.

Carron, A. V., Colman, M. M., Wheeler, J. and Stevens, D. (2002). Cohesion and performance in sport: A meta-analysis. *Journal of Sport & Exercise Psychology, 24,* 168–188.

Carron, A. V., Shapcott, K. M. and Burke, S. M. (2007). Group cohesion in sport and exercise: Past, present, and future. In M. R. Beauchamp and M. A. Eys (Eds), *Group dynamics in exercise and sport psychology* (pp. 117–141). London: Routledge.

Chelladurai, P. (2013). A personal journey in theorizing in sport management. *Sport Management Review, 16,* 22–28.

Jowett, S. (2007). Coach-athlete relationships ignite sense of groupness. In M. R. Beauchamp and M. A. Eys (Eds), *Group dynamics in exercise and sport psychology* (pp. 63–78). London: Routledge.

Karau, S. J. and Williams, K. D. (1993). Social loafing: A meta-analytic review and theoretical integration. *Journal of Personality and Social Psychology, 65,* 681–706.

Riemer, H. A. (2007). Multidimensional model of coach leadership. In S. Jowett and D. Lavallee (Eds), *Social psychology in sport* (pp. 57–73). Champaign, IL: Human Kinetics.

Ringelmann, M. (1913). Recherches sur les moteurs Anime's Travail de l'homme. *Annales de l'Institut National Agronomique, 12,* 1–40.

Tuckman, B. W. and Jensen, M. A. C. (1977). Stages of small group development revisited. *Group and Organizational Studies, 2,* 419–427.

PSYCHOLOGICAL SKILLS TRAINING

CHAPTER LEARNING OBJECTIVES

1 Overview psychological skills training.
2 Identify typical psychological characteristics associated with sport performance.
3 Examine common strategies used to build psychological characteristics.
4 Describe how psychological skills training programmes typically get delivered.
5 Detail what athletes should look for in effective sport psychologists.

One game into the season, Coach Taylor had to promote Matt to starting quarterback due to an injury to 'QB1'. Although Matt was a dedicated team player, who worked hard in practice, he was easily distracted during games, typically got anxious and could be hesitant in his decision-making. Coach had kept Matt on the roster over the last three seasons, however, because he had demonstrated a high level of skill and physical prowess for the sport. On many occasions over the last three years in training, warm-up games and competition, Coach had seen that when Matt 'put it together' or 'forgot himself' he could turn a game with devastating effect. Coach Taylor, however, had found his attempts to assist Matt had produced inconsistent results and he decided to see if a sport psychologist could help. He did not know any psychologists and so asked around the assistant coaches for referrals. One of the defensive coaches suggested a lady called Tammy, a local licensed psychologist, whose name had been mentioned by one of the players. The player said Tammy helped him with feelings of depression when he had not been recovering from an injury quickly enough. Although Coach Taylor did not understand how a psychologist worked and he thought the area was a bunch of mumbo jumbo, he wanted to find out if Tammy could help Matt. As always, Matt had been open to Coach Taylor's idea and booked an appointment.

Experienced sport psychologists will recognise the situation above and are often asked to help athletes when they are having difficulties. It is not always the case, however, that athletes approach practitioners only when they are in trouble. Clients also approach psychologists at other times, such as when they are playing well and want to get even better. Also, athletes and coaches may seek psychological assistant for difficulties seemingly unrelated to performance (e.g. relationship, gambling or mental health issues). The focus of this chapter is on the ways sport psychologists typically help athletes with performance enhancement. Although the methods in the current chapter may help with other issues, many times additional specialised knowledge and skills are needed, such as when working with athletes experiencing eating disorders or substance abuse. In these instances if practitioners do not have the skills, they are ethically obliged to refer clients to suitably trained professionals.

The divide between performance and other issues is often murky. Problems stemming from circumstances outside of sport may interfere with performance, for example, when athletes respond to bereavement with feelings of depression. Also, performance issues may have rippling effects beyond sport. Dependence on performance-enhancing drugs, for example, may give rise to health, relationship, social and occupational difficulties. The majority of performance-related issues, however, for which athletes seek psychological assistance can be helped by the strategies detailed below and are often grouped together under the label 'psychological skills training'. In this chapter I describe what psychological skills training typically involves, explain the common psychological characteristics and methods subsumed under the label and offer points for identifying the types of psychologists likely to help athletes effectively.

PSYCHOLOGICAL SKILLS TRAINING

Psychological skills training focuses on teaching athletes strategies to help them develop characteristics associated with enhanced performance. A key aspect of these psychologically oriented training programmes is the use of psychological methods with the purpose of developing psychological characteristics (Vealey 1994). An analogy can be drawn with strength training. Muscular strength contributes to superior performance in many sports, and weight-training is the common method used to build the attribute. Similarly, sometimes athletes experience motivational difficulties, because they cannot see a clear path to follow towards their dreams. Goal-setting (psychological method) may in these situations help athletes channel their motivation (psychological characteristic) to achieve. Figure 7.1 illustrates common psychological characteristics and methods written about in sport psychology, and also suggests that psychological factors are one of a number of influences on performance, along with physical and social variables.

Figure 7.1 proposes that psychological characteristics contribute to the 'ideal performance state', or that state of readiness involving both mental and physical components that allow athletes to perform to their best. From a psychological perspective, the ideal performance state involves having the 'right frame of mind' that allows athletes to be focused, confident and sufficiently energised to perform the skills they may have spent hours, weeks, months or years developing. The ideal performance state involves a balanced blend of physical, psychological and other attributes, and each may be considered necessary but insufficient for enhanced performance. Matt above, for example, seems like an athlete who has the physical attributes needed to perform well, but would likely benefit from developing some psychological characteristics, such as his confidence.

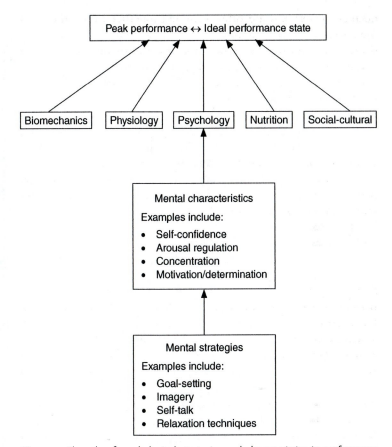

Figure 7.1: The role of psychological strategies and characteristics in performance enhancement.

Sport psychologists have largely borrowed the psychological strategies they use from the cognitive-behavioural therapy approach to clinical and counselling psychology (Beck 1995). One key idea in cognitive-behavioural therapy is that people's responses to events in their lives are influenced by their perceptions and beliefs. If people change their perceptions and beliefs then they can alter the way they respond to things that happen to them. Another key idea is that thoughts, feelings and behaviour influence each other, as illustrated in the discussion on self-efficacy in

Chapter 4. Self-efficacy influences performance, which is a behaviour. In turn, performance (labelled as mastery experiences) is a source of self-efficacy. Coaches and athletes typically share similar beliefs: the ways individuals think and feel influence their training and performance. In turn, the way that athletes perform in competition and training can change their thoughts and feelings (e.g. raise or dampen their self-beliefs, anxieties and determination). In cognitive-behavioural therapy, the psychological strategies practitioners use help modify clients' perceptions, beliefs, emotions and behaviours so that they can resolve and manage their issues. Similarly, the psychological strategies sport psychologists use help athletes modify their perceptions, states, feelings and beliefs (psychological characteristics) so that they can enhance their training and performance.

TYPICAL PSYCHOLOGICAL CHARACTERISTICS ASSOCIATED WITH SPORT PERFORMANCE

In Figure 7.1, peak performance refers to episodes of superior functioning, involving the display of skill levels that may be above athletes' normal levels of play and often result in new personal bests (Kane and Williams, 2010). Over the years, sport psychologists have: (a) asked athletes to describe their peak experiences; (b) compared successful and unsuccessful athletes on their psychological characteristics; and (c) investigated how psychological qualities differ between athletes' good and poor performances. Across these studies, common psychological characteristics have emerged as illustrated in Table 7.1. Researchers have also examined the psychological

Table 7.1: Psychological characteristics associated with enhanced athletic performance

High self-confidence, expectations of success and beliefs of being in control
Self-regulation of arousal
Total concentration and focus on the present task
Viewing difficult situations as exciting and challenging
Having high but flexible standards
Positive thoughts about performance
Strong determination and commitment

Source: Based on Krane and Williams (2010).

characteristics associated with poor performance and have found that many are the opposite of those attributes in Table 7.1, including self-doubts, acting differently to normal, focusing on irrelevant information, overemphasising the outcome or other factors outside the athlete's control, over- or under-arousal and interpreting situations as threatening or harmful. The identification of psychological characteristics associated with good and poor performance provides one justification for using mental strategies. Sport psychologists, for example, want to help athletes to develop these characteristics so they can achieve enhanced performance and attain their sporting goals.

TYPICAL STRATEGIES USED TO ENHANCE PSYCHOLOGICAL CHARACTERISTICS

Figure 7.1 also lists examples of psychological strategies individuals can use to enhance the psychological characteristics associated with peak performance. There are a great many more that could have been included, but those listed are ones athletes commonly use and for which there is some evidence they enhance skill execution. These techniques may also help athletes develop other characteristics associated with enhanced performance. For example, research has indicated that imagery can promote the development of muscular strength.

Although psychological strategies can benefit athletes, they cannot compensate entirely for poor physical training, inadequate technique or unsuitable dietary practices. Instead, optimal performance results from a synergy of the various factors (Hodge 2004). Goal-setting is a good example, because it helps individuals maximise their physical training. In the absence of physical training, goal-setting does not lead to improved conditioning. Without effective goal-setting, individuals may not maximise their training gains. Together, effective goal-setting and optimal physical training allows athletes to reach their potential. In the following sections the common psychological strategies sport psychologists use are described. Specifically, I describe the essence of the strategy, why it can help athletes and insights into how individuals can use the technique.

GOAL-SETTING

WHAT IS GOAL-SETTING?

Goal-setting is a process whereby athletes: (a) identify what they want to achieve; (b) plan how they will obtain these aims; (c) set target dates for attainment; (d) work towards their objectives; and (e) evaluate their progress. Many athletes have goals, but do not engage in goal-setting. Some of these individuals may achieve their goals because of other reasons, such as inherited abilities or good coaching, but goal-setting provides athletes with a process by which they can work towards their dreams in a proactive fashion.

WHY MIGHT GOAL-SETTING HELP ATHLETES?

Locke and Latham's (2002) well-respected theory explains why goal-setting may help athletes. First, goals direct people's attention towards the relevant activities that allow them to achieve their objectives. Second, goal-setting leads to increased effort and motivation, because people have a clear idea of what they have to do and what they want to achieve. Third, goals influence persistence. Fourth, goals lead to the creation and use of relevant learning or problem-solving strategies.

HOW MIGHT ATHLETES USE GOAL-SETTING?

Table 7.2 presents a framework that can help coaches and athletes use goal-setting. The framework assists athletes to plan what they want, start working towards their goals and review and modify their attempts to make them more effective. With following the framework, there are some guidelines athletes can follow to help increase goal-setting's effectiveness.

- *Set difficult, specific, but achievable goals.* Increasing goal difficulty leads to improved performance until the limits of ability are reached or goal commitment is lost. Moderately difficult goals are associated with best performance compared with easy or unrealistic objectives. In addition, specific goals ('increase jump height by 2 cm') lead to greater performance consistency

Table 7.2: A goal-setting framework for athletes

Stage 1: Determine athletes' long-term aims

For example, being selected for a particular team, going to the Olympics, having fun

Stage 2: Identify the specific attributes needed to attain the long-term goal

For example, physical, psychological, social or other attributes

Stage 3: Detail a plan for achieving the long- and short-term goals

Develop a programme for achieving the goals being as specific as possible. Also identify barriers to goal achievement and develop strategies to overcome them

Stage 4: Implement the plan

The only way to know if it works is to try it!

Stage 5: Regularly review progress

Initial planning may not result in the optimal programme, but regular evaluation may help make the programme more effective

---

because they stipulate a standard of achievement more clearly than vague goals ('jump higher'). Together, specific, difficult, but realistic goals lead to greater and more consistent performance than vague and easy or unrealistic goals.

- *Set different types of goals.* Setting different types of goals appears more helpful than focusing on one kind of target. Athletes, for example, can set outcome, performance and process targets (Hardy and Jones, 1994). Outcome goals focus on the results of social comparisons, such as the finishing order in a competition. Performance goals identify standards of achievement independent of other people, such as improving one's personal best in an event. Process goals detail behaviours that individuals will focus on during training and competition, such as keeping the bar close to the legs during a deadlift. Outcome goals can have tremendous motivational value because they may encapsulate the reasons why athletes are involved in their sports ('I want to win an Olympic gold medal!'). Performance and process goals help provide a plan to ensure athletes work towards their dreams.
- *Set short-term and long-term goals.* Long-term goals provide individuals with direction. Short-term goals help to break a long-term target into achievable steps. Using both short- and long-term goals is more helpful than using either on their own.
- *Develop goal achievement strategies.* Setting a goal becomes goal-setting when athletes identify how they are going to achieve

their goals. Developing goal achievement strategies helps focus athletes' efforts towards useful actions and behaviours.

* *Develop ways to ensure feedback.* In sport it is often possible for athletes to obtain immediate and unambiguous feedback about their performance. Strategies that capitalise on this feature help improve goal-setting effectiveness and athletes' self-awareness. Individuals who know themselves and their current limits can set challenging yet realistic goals and they can modify their current achievement strategies to be more helpful.

Table 7.3 provides a goal-setting plan a junior power-lifter followed in the build-up to a competition. The plan illustrates long- and short-term goals, along with outcome, performance

Table 7.3: A novice power-lifter's training plan

Outcome goal:	To win club competition		
Performance goals:	Total 595 kg, 220 squat, 140 bench press, 235 deadlift		

Short-term training goals (kg × reps)

Week	Squat	Bench	Deadlift
1	100 × 10	75 × 10	115 ×10
2	110 × 10	80 × 10	125 × 10
3	120 × 8	85 × 8	135 × 8
4	130 × 8	90 × 8	145 × 8
5	140 × 6	195 × 6	155 × 6
6	150 × 6	100 × 6	165 × 6
7	160 × 5	105 × 5	175 × 5
8	170 × 5	110 × 5	185 × 5
9	180 × 4	115 × 4	195 × 4
10	190 × 4	120 × 4	205 × 4
11	200 × 3	125 × 3	215 × 3
12	210 × 2	130 × 2	225 × 2

Competitive performance goals

	Squat	Bench	Deadlift
1st lift	210	130	215
2nd lift	215	137.5	225
3rd lift	220	140	235

Competitive process goals

Squat	'Tight and explode'
Bench press	'Drive the eyes'
Deadlift	'Through the hips'

and process goals. The lifter had kept training and competition records for the previous three years and so was able to set specific and moderately challenging goals. The plan fitted on a single sheet of A4 paper and was pinned to the athlete's bedroom wall. Each day before and after training he would review his plan and make adjustments as needed, illustrating how he engaged in regular review. The example also illustrates that goal-setting can be straightforward and uncomplicated.

The influence of goal-setting on behaviour and performance, including athletic endeavours, is one of the most robust findings in psychological literature, paralleling the common belief that a clear idea of your desires and how you can attain them contributes to success in many achievement domains (Kyllo and Landers 1995). Based on these beliefs and scientific evidence it is understandable that goal-setting is often one of the strategies sport psychologists employ first. A second common strategy is imagery.

IMAGERY

WHAT IS IMAGERY?

Imagery is a mental process involving multisensory experiences in the absence of actual perception. For example, weight-trainers might 'see' a barbell above their heads even though they have no equipment. They may also 'feel' the weight pushing down on their hands and the tension in their bodies. They might also 'hear' their laboured breathing and their training partners yelling, encouraging them to keep going. Effective imagery includes each of the senses related to performance: visual, tactile, auditory, etc. Imagery has been a popular area of research and much evidence reveals it increases skill execution and learning.

WHY MIGHT IMAGERY HELP ATHLETES?

Although many explanations for imagery's effectiveness exist, in recent years the functional equivalence hypothesis (Jeannerod, 1995) has gained acceptance in sport psychology. The hypothesis proposes that imagery shares similar neural features with physical motor task preparation and execution. For example, research indicates the same brain areas are active when imaging or physically performing a task. Imagery allows athletes to prepare and plan for a movement by accessing, strengthening and refining the same neural pathways of the movement as when physically performing (Murphy *et al.* 2008).

WAYS ATHLETES CAN USE IMAGERY

Functional equivalence, however, is not an automatic consequence of imagery. Holmes and Collins' (2001) PETTLEP model helps athletes create the types of images that will be functionally equivalent and effective in enhancing skill execution:

- *Physical.* Imagery is more effective if athletes replicate the physical movements and other aspects associated with competition. For example, they can move during imagery, hold equipment, wear competitive clothing and act as if they were competing.
- *Environment.* Individuals can mimic the competitive environment as much as possible, perhaps even undertaking imagery at the actual location. If they cannot visit the actual location, they can use videos, photographs and descriptions from others who have performed at the arena to enhance imagery.
- *Task.* Focusing on the same things and employing the same senses athletes use during competition enhances functional equivalence. One particular sense is the kinaesthetic sense or the feeling of movement. Athletes often find that their movements feel grooved or 'right' when performing well. Being able to recreate that grooved feeling during imagery may well help enhance functional equivalence. To help, athletes might say the same self-talk cues during imagery that they do during performance.
- *Timing.* Generally, functional equivalence will be more likely to result if athletes imagine performing the task at the same speed as they do physically than if they visualise it faster or slower. Occasionally, however, changing imagery speed may be beneficial. Imaging movements slowly, for example, may allow the analysis of technique. In these situations, maintaining movement rhythm may help maintain functional equivalence.
- *Learning.* With learning, the way athletes move and react to cues changes (see Chapter 8). For example, their movements may be jerky when first learning a task but they may become

more efficient as they practice. During periods of skill development, adjusting imagery content so it mirrors how athletes react and move will enhance functional equivalence.

- *Emotion.* Effective imagery includes the emotions and arousal levels athletes experience when physically performing. Sometimes professionals may recommend that sports people relax when doing imagery. In most sporting situations, however, athletes do not wish to be overly relaxed and may be best advised to avoid combining imagery with relaxation unless there is a specific purpose.
- *Perspective.* Athletes can use internal or external imagery. During internal imagery, individuals perceive the task as they would if actually performing the movement ('through their own eyes'). In external imagery, individuals perceive the task from the third person ('watching themselves on video'). Both perspectives can be beneficial. The one employed needs to match athletes' preferences and the task demands. For example, an internal perspective may be suitable for open-skill sports where success depends on perception and reacting to environmental cues.

There are various reasons athletes might use imagery, including practising technique, correcting mistakes, preparing for competition, enhancing self-efficacy and stress management. The PETTLEP model can assist athletes to select helpful images. Furthermore, they can develop and record imagery scripts (descriptions athletes use to guide an imagery session). Scripts can consist of words, symbols, pictures or video recordings. One weightlifter's script, for example, had a series of stick-figure diagrams with red arrows indicting body-part movements. The arrows were red because she associated the colour with high levels of arousal and she wanted to be highly activated when she performed. The stick-figures helped her adopt an external perspective because she needed to maintain correct technique to succeed.

Imagery has been a popular method among sport psychologists and athletes, perhaps because it is intuitive that many things are created twice: first mentally (even if subconsciously) and then physically. Imagery helps athletes harness such a principle.

Whereas imagery focuses on images, another common technique, self-talk, focuses on the words athletes tell themselves.

SELF-TALK

WHAT IS SELF-TALK?

Self-talk refers to statements, said out loud or quietly, addressed to the self for a specific purpose, such as a sprinter who says 'explode' at the start line. Self-talk can be positive ('I can do well'), negative ('I will do badly'), instructional ('keep my head down'), or motivational ('success will be great'). Self-talk improves skill execution and learning across different athletes and sports. Although positive self-talk improves skill execution, negative self-talk does not always impede performance, because some athletes use their negative inner dialogue to motivate themselves.

WHY MIGHT SELF-TALK LEAD TO IMPROVED SKILL EXECUTION?

Researchers have not demonstrated conclusively why self-talk works, although it may help individuals: (a) concentrate on relevant cues; (b) enhance their motivation; (c) produce efficient movement patterns; or (d) manage their emotions. The best current evidence is that self-talk enhances technique and assists athletes with their concentration. Most likely, however, there is no single reason why self-talk works, rather it is a combination of the four reasons above (Tod *et al.* 2011).

WAYS THAT ATHLETES MAY USE SELF-TALK

Similar to the other psychological skills training methods, athletes will benefit most from self-talk if they identify the purpose for using it. One rugby union player, for example, used the phrase 'dominate this channel' at every defensive scrum to focus on his task of stopping any opposition attack on his side of the field. The typical reasons athletes use self-talk include learning and ensuring good technique, mentally preparing for skill execution and enhancing the various psychological characteristics associated with good performance (e.g. self-confidence, motivation and concentration).

Landin (1994) provided guidelines for developing suitable self-talk statements. First, keep phrases short, perhaps to one or two words. Second, use cues logically associated with the task. Third, ensure the information in the verbal statements is meaningful to athletes. Fourth, consider the type of task being performed. For example, many sporting tasks involve several components that need to be blended in a rapid and smooth manner. In such cases, self-talk cues that direct athletes' attention to movement outcomes may be more suitable than instructional statements (say 'get high' rather than 'bend and drive' during jumping activities). Fifth, consider athletes' skill level or familiarity with the task. Simple instructional self-talk may be suitable for novices, whereas motivational cues might be suited to well-trained athletes.

Self-talk may be most helpful when included as part of routines athletes use regularly or have practised for unusual situations. The rugby union player above provides an example of self-talk being incorporated in a routine fashion. As another example, a golfer found it helpful to identify something she did well after every shot, so that when she had a poor stroke she was in the habit of looking for something positive. Doing so helped her stay upbeat for the next shot. Frequently, things do not always go smoothly, and self-talk may help athletes adjust. After being hit in the chest when batting, for example, a cricketer used the cue 'nose in line' as the bowler delivered the ball to stay focused on the present rather than remember being struck.

In addition to the other uses identified, imagery and self-talk can help athletes control their stress, anxiety and arousal levels. Although sometimes athletes need to increase their arousal, more commonly they benefit from reducing them, and sport psychologists can teach individuals how to relax.

RELAXATION TECHNIQUES

WHAT ARE RELAXATION TECHNIQUES?

Relaxation strategies are designed to help athletes reduce their physical and cognitive arousal to the levels needed for optimal performance. Among the numerous strategies, some focus on reducing physiological arousal. Progressive muscular relaxation is an example and involves the tensing and relaxing of body parts (lower legs, upper legs, buttocks, etc.). Other strategies are designed to help reduce cognitive anxieties and meditation is an example in which individuals clear their mind by focusing on a mantra or a single thought. Behavioural or multimodal strategies help athletes: (a) reduce physiological and cognitive arousal; and (b) develop skills to cope with stressful circumstances. During stress inoculation training, for example, people develop and rehearse behaviours and skills they then use in stressful situations. Relaxation techniques, however, do not typically reduce just either physiological or cognitive arousal. The mind and body are interconnected, and most methods lead to reductions in both types of activation.

WHY MIGHT RELAXATION TECHNIQUES HELP ATHLETES?

In Chapter 3 I discussed possible reasons why increased physiological and cognitive arousal past optimal levels may impair performance: the increased muscle tension may interfere with movement coordination, and heightened cognitive arousal may lead to attention narrowing and shifting from relevant to irrelevant cues. Relaxation techniques may help athletes regain movement control and attention focus. Individuals may find coordination improves and they can focus once again on relevant cues.

HOW MIGHT ATHLETES USE RELAXATION TECHNIQUES?

It is beneficial for athletes to have several relaxation and coping strategies at their disposal, because they suit different situations. Techniques, for example, that allow athletes to attain deep relaxation levels often take several minutes or more to implement. These strategies are useful the night before a game or as part of a build-up, but generally are not helpful during an event. Methods that are quick to implement may be helpful during a competition, but athletes typically do not relax as much as with other strategies. Normally, however, athletes do not want to relax too deeply during an event! If athletes are proficient in several techniques, they can select the method suitable for the situation they are experiencing.

Centring is an example that takes 2-3 seconds to implement and can be used during competitive events. When centring, athletes control their breathing and use key phrases to clear their thoughts. The following is one illustrative exercise:

- Stand with your feet shoulder-width apart, arms by your side and head up.
- Hold your upper body erect.
- Breathe in, lift your shoulders and expand your chest and stomach. Feel the rise in tension in your upper body.
- Hold your breath for about 1-2 seconds.
- Breathe out and let your shoulders, chest and stomach return to their normal position.
- Say to yourself 'relax' and notice the tension drop away into the floor.

Athletes can practice centring throughout their daily lives until they are able to reduce their arousal and clear their thoughts. As they become accustomed to using the strategy they can implement it in training and competition. One way to implement centring is to identify specific moments in an event where it would help, such as at the free throw line in basketball, prior to release in archery, or just before a penalty kick in many team sports.

I hope the above discussion illustrates ways in which sport psychology is an applied science focused on helping athletes resolve their concerns or achieve their dreams. There is a large body of literature about the techniques and I have only provided a snapshot of each. The References list provides excellent resources if more information is wanted.

HOW PSYCHOLOGICAL SKILLS TRAINING PROGRAMMES ARE TYPICALLY DELIVERED

The process by which sport psychologists help athletes often includes a series of steps including: assessment and objective setting; identification of suitable interventions; implementation; and review. The process might take many sessions over an extended period of time, such as in the build-up to a World Championship or an Olympic Games. Alternatively, the process may be curtailed and occur briefly over 5-10 minutes, such as when practitioners help athletes in crisis shortly before an event.

During assessment, practitioners make use of various tools, such as interviews, questionnaires, behaviour observations or physiological measurements, to identify what attributes athletes need help to develop. For example, through talking as they walked around a course, a practitioner and golfer decided that developing confidence and learning to relax would help him manage anger after a mistake. As a result of undertaking a needs assessment, the client and practitioner set objectives to guide the rest of the process.

The next step is to identify suitable solutions, strategies, or interventions. Sport psychologists commonly use the above interventions and many others, such as music, role-plays and hypnosis. Psychologists may explore ways athletes have coped with challenges in the past and if possible, help them apply these strategies to current issues. For example, if an athlete has previously found certain self-talk cues helpful in coping with pre-competition anxieties, then she and the practitioner might discuss how to reuse similar phrases in upcoming events.

There are often two parts to implementing sport psychology interventions. Initially, athletes may benefit from learning the strategy to become comfortable with the method. Once athletes are comfortable with the tactic, they can then begin using it in training and low-stress events before employing it in high-pressure situations. When using imagery, for example, athletes might undertake homework exercises to develop the quality and controllability of their images, before using it to enhance performance. Athletes who do not control their imagery may imagine themselves making mistakes and performing poorly, leading to reduced self-belief, persistence and performance.

Reviewing intervention effectiveness allows athletes to continue to use, modify, or stop using the strategy. Modifying useful strategies, for example, can help increase their efficacy. To illustrate, a rugby union player who had found visualisation useful began having imagery sessions with a teammate with whom she needed a close relationship during competition for the team to be successful (they were the team's flyhalf and scrumhalf). The athlete found that her level of play improved as she and her teammate spent time walking around the field imaging how they would work together in game-specific scenarios.

Tailoring interventions to athletes' needs and circumstances helps them gain the most from psychological skills training programmes. There are 'one size fits all' programmes available from practitioners and the internet. Although such packages may help some athletes with specific issues, such 'canned' programmes are unlikely to be helpful for the majority of athletes and probably only moderately helpful for a few.

WHAT SHOULD ATHLETES LOOK FOR IN EFFECTIVE SPORT PSYCHOLOGISTS?

There are many applied sport psychology books and resources from which athletes and coaches can learn about the strategies above. Some athletes find these resources helpful in enhancing performance. Other athletes benefit from a sport psychologist's assistance. Effective sport psychologists can help athletes clarify their needs and tailor strategies to their circumstances (Tod and Andersen 2005). Such two-way interaction is not available with a book.

Effective applied sport psychology is based on a collaborative relationship. Athletes and practitioners work together to help clients achieve their goals. Such collaborative relationships have three dimensions. First, there is agreement on the goals to be pursued and these aims are client-driven ('learn to manage anger on the golf course'). Sometimes athletes approach practitioners knowing what they want to achieve, sometimes they need help clarifying their aims and sometimes these targets change over time. Regardless, however, the goals are identified and are in clients' interests. Second, there is agreement on each person's responsibilities. For example, practitioners may be tasked with providing psychological space for athletes to explore their issues and solutions, as well as helping them apply strategies in useful ways. Athletes may be tasked with being willing to confront their limitations and undertake 'homework' exercises. Third, ideally both parties like, trust and respect each other and there is a strong interpersonal bond. If, for example, athletes do not feel respected by practitioners then they may refrain from sharing relevant personal information. Understanding that collaborative relationships are the foundation of effective applied sport psychology can help athletes identify suitable practitioners. Some researchers have asked athletes to describe the characteristics of effective sport psychologists with the following results.

Helpful practitioners have high levels of technical competence, including a range of psychological interventions they can apply to specific situations. They also know how and why interventions work and can tailor them to athletes' needs. Effective practitioners learn about athletes' needs and situations and then use that information to adapt interventions to clients' circumstances. Athletes can ask potential practitioners about their qualifications and professional status. Knowing that a practitioner has professional recognition, such as being a certified consultant with the Association for the Advancement of Sport Psychology in the USA or being registered with the Health and Care Professions Council in the UK, gives athletes some assurance that the person has the necessary technical competencies to deliver sport psychology services. Athletes can also ask practitioners to describe how they operate and their experience with the sport. Providing clear answers about how they operate in ways athletes understand and using examples from the sport may indicate an ability to apply psychological interventions in effective ways.

Also, helpful practitioners have strong interpersonal and counselling skills. They are empathetic and care about their clients. Athletes can ask themselves if they 'click' with and trust the individual. It may take more than one session to establish such an interpersonal bond, but if after several sessions mutual trust and respect are not developing, then service delivery outcomes may be compromised. More specific questions athletes can ask themselves include: is the practitioner treating me as an expert in my sport? Does the practitioner listen? Does the individual care? Is the practitioner friendly (but does not try to be a friend)? Does the practitioner have my best interests at heart? Has the practitioner addressed important issues such as confidentiality?

In collaborative relationships, positive outcomes result from the combined efforts of all parties. The likelihood of getting the benefits from working with consultants is increased if athletes adopt a positive realistic attitude. If athletes do not believe that interventions will be helpful, they may not practice them as needed. Also, it may take time before interventions lead to benefits. The exact amount of time varies according to the intervention or desired outcome. For example, self-talk may yield relatively quick results in helping direct athletes' attention to task-relevant cues. In contrast, athletes may need to spend considerable time to develop, implement, evaluate and modify a well-constructed effective goal-setting plan.

CONCLUSION

Returning to Coach Taylor and Matt, it is likely that Tammy will undertake a procedure mirroring this chapter's content. She probably will conduct a needs assessment to identify the psychological (and other) attributes and methods that will help Matt believe in himself, control his anxieties and make decisions under pressure. This might include, for example, overlearning drills so he can react automatically during a game. Tammy might also use imagery, relaxation techniques, performance routines or other psychological techniques in her armamentarium of interventions. If Matt engages fully in the process and the two individuals establish a strong collaborative relationship, then Coach Taylor may be surprised by the results and learn that psychology is not all mumbo-jumbo.

REFERENCES

Beck, J. S. (1995). *Cognitive therapy: Basics and beyond.* New York: Guilford Press.

Hardy, L. and Jones, G. (1994). Current issues and future directions for performance-related research in sport psychology. *Journal of Sports Sciences, 12*, 61-92.

Hodge, K. (2004). *Sport motivation: Training your mind for peak performance.* Auckland, New Zealand: Reed.

Holmes, P. S. and Collins, D. J. (2001). The PETTLEP approach to motor imagery: A functional equivalence model for sport psychologists. *Journal of Applied Sport Psychology, 13*, 60-83.

Jeannerod, M. (1995). Mental imagery in the motor context. *Neuropsychologia, 33*, 1419–1432.

Krane, V. and Williams, J. M. (2010). Psychological characteristics of peak performance. In J. M. Williams (Ed.), *Applied sport psychology: Personal growth to peak performance* (6th ed., pp. 169–188). Boston: McGraw Hill.

Kyllo, L. B. and Landers, D. M. (1995). Goal setting in sport and exercise: A research synthesis to resolve the controversy. *Journal of Sport & Exercise Psychology, 17*, 117–137.

Landin, D. (1994). The role of verbal cues in skill learning. *Quest, 46*, 299–313.

Locke, E. A. and Latham, G. P. (2002). Building a practically useful theory of goal setting and task motivation: A 35-year odyssey. *American Psychologist, 57*, 705–717.

Murphy, S., Nordin, S. and Cumming, J. (2008). Imagery in sport, exercise, and dance. In T. S. Horn (Ed.), *Advances in sport psychology* (3rd ed., pp. 297–324). Champaign, IL: Human Kinetics.

Tod, D. and Andersen, M. B. (2005). Effective sport psycholoigsts. In S. Murphy (Ed.), *The sport psych handbook* (pp. 305–314). Champaign, IL: Human Kinetics.

Tod, D., Hardy, J. and Oliver, E. (2011). Effects of self-talk: A systematic review. *Journal of Sport & Exercise Psychology, 33*, 666–687.

Vealey, R. S. (1994). Current status and prominent issues in sport psychology interventions. *Medicine and Science in Sports and Exercise, 26*, 495–502.

PHYSICAL SKILLS TRAINING

CHAPTER LEARNING OUTCOMES

1 Explore the stages through which athletes proceed as they learn new skills.
2 Discuss ways coaches might structure practice to optimise skill-learning.
3 Review principles of behaviour modification.
4 Detail how extrinsic feedback might be delivered to assist learning.

Coach Lance Sweets has just taken charge of the Jeffersonian School under-12-year-old mixed rugby union team. Coach Sweets is a professional psychologist who has never coached previously, although he played a great deal of sport himself when growing up. He had been a talented rugby player and had enjoyed the physical contact of the game. He was looking forward to being involved in the sport once again. When meeting the squad at the first team practice, however, he realised that he was unsure how to teach the players the technical aspects of the game, such as passing, catching and tackling. He had an idea of the skills involved, but did not know how to communicate those thoughts to the players or the best way to set up drills and exercises. Perhaps due to his hesitancy, he also found that some of the players started misbehaving. In particular, several of the team were picking on one boy, Jack, because he had red hair. Several players were calling him names related to his hair colour, and Jack reacted by getting angry and started trying to push the other boys around physically. Lance spent several minutes calming Jack down, and as he did so the other players stopped practising and started playing 'chicken' by throwing balls at each other. One player, Seeley, threw a ball that hit one of the female team members, Angela, in the shoulder when she was not looking. Lance sent Seeley on a run around the field and then managed to regain control of the team by yelling at the players, before getting them to finish practice with a game of touch rugby. After training, Angela and another female player, Temperance, approached Lance saying they were thinking of quitting because Seeley was always picking on them and making them feel like they should not be on the team. Lance replied that they had every right to be on the team and that he would deal with Seeley. He also mentioned that they looked like they had some talent and that he hoped they would stay on the team. Later that night over dinner with his partner Daisy, Lance thought he needed to learn how to structure training so that the team would stay focused on learning the skills needed to play both as individuals and as a team. He thought that this might also help him control the players' behaviour, especially Jack and Seeley, whom he thought had misbehaved because he didn't keep them busy. Daisy asked if any of Lance's psychology training might help.

Responsible sport psychologists adhere to professional codes of ethics so that the services they provide are of high quality, are within their realms of expertise and are delivered in ways that respects clients' dignity and welfare. Where possible, such psychologists also ensure their services are not compromised as a result of being in dual relationships with their clients (e.g. being a psychologist and a sports coach at the same time). If Coach Sweets avoids engaging the children with his sport psychologist hat on, then he will maintain rather than violate professional boundary issues.

Sport psychologists also often work in multidisciplinary teams. For example, the support team for a professional sports club might include a head coach, several assistant coaches, a sport psychologist, an exercise physiologist, one or more trainers, a nutritionist and possibly a massage therapist. In these situations sport psychologists respect the boundaries of their own and others' roles in a team. For example, sport psychologists are employed to offer psychological services and not to coach. Although similarities exist, the two roles are different. Nevertheless, sport psychologists have studied topics related to coaching, such as skill-learning, behaviour modification and leadership (see Chapter 6). The knowledge generated may help coaches achieve their aims. In the above vignette, the information and techniques Coach Sweets learned in his training could help him develop the players' physical skills and modify their behaviour. In this chapter I will discuss: (a) the stages athletes proceed through when learning skills; (b) issues that coaches might find helpful when structuring skills training sessions; (c) principles of behaviour modification; and (d) the role of feedback in performance improvement.

STAGES OF LEARNING

One way that psychologists have contributed to understanding skill-learning is by examining the changes that occur as individuals become proficient in a task. A well-known skill-learning framework is Fitts and Posner's (1967) three-stage model. Although the three stages are presented here as discrete phases, they are points along a continuum. It is difficult to determine exactly when individuals have moved from one stage to the next.

The first or cognitive stage occurs when people start learning a skill. Individuals engage in a large amount of cognitive activity as they attempt to develop mental maps or an understanding of the movement. They are focused on questions such as 'what am I trying to achieve?' 'Where do I place my body?' 'What is the best posture?' During performance they may also attempt to coach themselves through the movement. Skill execution is highly variable and there is limited consistency. Learners make large and frequent errors which can stimulate frustration. They also have limited self-awareness and may not know if they are developing bad habits or doing something incorrectly. If they are aware something is wrong, they may not know what to do. For example, a novice cricket batter may be unaware that anxiety is causing her to move her back foot away as a fast bowler delivers a ball, and a coach may need to place a brick behind her feet to help her realise this tendency. The coach can also advise on how to remain stable and balanced, because the batter will probably not know how to remedy her habit.

Athletes enter the second or associative stage once they have developed a mental map of the movement. They may also have begun to associate environmental cues with the necessary movements to be successful, such as cricket batters who may adjust their technique or shot selection based on cues from the bowler. Skill refinement is a major change during the associative stage, and there are improvements in performance level and consistency. Errors occur less frequently and are smaller in magnitude. Athletes may also begin to develop an ability to detect and correct some of their own performance errors. The cricket batter from above may start to recognise when her back foot slides and may use her coach's advice about how to stay stable.

After considerable practice, some athletes enter the third or autonomous stage. Performance is both high and consistent with few errors. The skill has become habitual and automatic with little or no conscious thought. Not every athlete reaches the autonomous stage. Those who do are able to do other things when performing, such as adjusting to environmental cues or communicating with teammates. Autonomous individuals are self-aware, as illustrated by their ability to detect and correct errors. During a cricket game, for example, proficient batters who are called out by the umpire will be able to identify their mistakes and will know what they need to do next time they are in the same situation.

As athletes become skilled, conscious processing drops, movement becomes automatic and their ability to detect and correct errors improves. Other changes also occur across the three stages (Magill, 2011). First, athletes' coordination improves and they overcome movement biases learned from similar but different skills. For example, learners may move the hand and forearm together as one unit and fail to produce a flick from the wrist as desired in some racket sports. Second, with progression individuals use less energy, increase movement efficiency and respond better to the environment, as illustrated by skilled athletes who appear to have all the time in the world to perform. Third, experts are able to direct their vision to features in the environment most likely to contain useful information, whereas learners tend to focus on too many cues, some of which are irrelevant. Experts are also able to initiate their visual searches earlier than novice performers. Fourth, experts have greater understanding of the activity, meaning they can solve problems and make decisions quicker than learners. As a result, experts are better able to anticipate opposition moves and read a game compared with novices. Fifth, the rate of improvement athletes experience decreases as they become more skilled, perhaps because there is less room for development. It takes greater effort and time to obtain a smaller increase in skill level for experts compared with novices who typically experience large improvements relatively quickly.

TRAINING DECISIONS

Understanding the changes that occur with skill-learning can help coaches make decisions about how to structure practice sessions to ensure progression. For example, coaches might consider the amount of variation to build into drills, how to distribute sessions, the amount of training needed to devote to a task and whether to practise the whole skill or just parts of the movement. Psychologists have conducted a large body of research that can assist coaches in making these decisions. (See books by Magill (2011) and Schmidt and Wrisberg (2008), who review the research underpinning material in the following sections.) One theme emerging from this research is that errors need not be considered a reflection of poor learning. Sometimes when psychologists have compared different practice regimes they have found that one schedule might yield better performance during the training session, but poorer results at a subsequent testing session (i.e., a lower transfer or retention of learning). In sport, athletes train so they can compete successfully at a later date, so from a coaching perspective, practice regimes associated with good skill transfer or retention are desirable. These findings also indicate that despite errors in training, athletes may still be learning and may still perform well in competition. Instead, errors might signal ways to improve performance.

TRAINING VARIATION

One question coaches may consider concerns the degree of variation to include in a training session. Although variation helps keep athletes engaged in training and avoid boredom, too much variation may interfere with learning, depending on the skill and athlete. Generally, research has shown that variation can be associated with enhanced learning if coaches make informed decisions about what and how much to vary.

One dimension coaches can vary is the context in which the skill is performed. Sport is played in many contexts, for example, in different weather conditions, on various surfaces and in front of different crowds. Evidence supports the suggestion that coaches should vary those aspects in training that are likely to differ in competition and keep constant those aspects that will not change.

Coaches can also vary the way they organise the practice of specific skills. For example, if Lance above wants to teach the players three variations of tackling he could use blocked or distributed practice. In blocked practice, he would teach one variation per session. If there were three training sessions a week, then once a week players would practise each type of tackle. There is variation across, but not within, a session. As an alternative, in distributed practice during each session athletes spend time on the three variations but the drill order is random. Blocked practice is associated with low contextual interference. Random distributed practice is associated with high contextual interference. Contextual interference refers to the interference resulting from practising variations of a skill within a session. For example, in dance sport, inexperienced athletes may find interference when switching between dances if different timings are used (e.g. going from a 4/4 to a 3/4 tempo). Interference, however, created from randomly practising several skill variations per session leads to higher retention of ability compared with blocked practice. Although researchers have demonstrated this contextual inference effect, it may not hold in all situations. For example, low-skilled athletes may benefit from blocked practice until they have developed proficiency at the movement. Based on these results, for example, coaches could plan to mix up training to provide adequate variation but remain flexible enough to move to a more blocked regime if athletes demonstrate a specific skill deficit.

TRAINING SESSION DISTRIBUTION

A second question that coaches might consider is how to distribute the time they have to teach athletes a skill. Often there are externally imposed time limits, such as needing to learn or improve a skill by a specific date or contest. When there is flexibility, however, two issues arise: (a) whether to have fewer longer or more frequent shorter practices; and (b) the length of the rest between skill attempts within a session. When considering the frequency and length of practice, the research generally suggests that shorter and more frequent training sessions are associated with better learning and retention of motor skills. For example, one-hour sessions every day may be preferable to practices of two hours every second day.

With respect to the rest period between skill attempts, a massed practice schedule is one where the amount of rest between attempts is short or non-existent. A distributed schedule involves a relatively long rest between trials (e.g. equal or more time is spent resting compared with practising a skill). If the skill being learned is continuous then best learning may arise from a distributed practice schedule where athletes rest between trials. Although much less research has been undertaken with respect to discrete skills, massed practice schedules appear preferable for learning and retention.

THE VALUE OF OVERLEARNING

The common chant of '10,000 hours and 10 years' is uttered by people to indicate that vast amounts of practice are needed to become an expert in a sport or any other domain. Such a mantra has emerged from the work of Ericsson (2007) and his colleagues on deliberate practice. Although it is correct to state that to become an expert requires intense deliberate training and mentoring over many years, coaches are often not aiming to produce experts, but instead are helping athletes achieve some level of proficiency in a much shorter time period. For example, some coaches only have a group of athletes for a year. Other coaches may have to help athletes achieve a specified standard of performance in preparation for a competition, grading or exam (e.g. in martial arts, gymnastics or dance sport). In these situations, research focused on overlearning a skill may be helpful. Overlearning involves extra practice after a proficiency standard has been achieved.

Coaches and athletes sometimes believe 'more is better' with skill-learning, and evidence reveals that overlearning is effective for retention, but there appears to be a point of diminishing returns. With experience, coaches may develop a sense for how much extra practice is worthwhile, but the different rates at which athletes learn a skill may limit how precise they can be in their estimations.

WHOLE VERSUS PART PRACTICE

Another relevant issue for coaches is whether to adopt a whole or part approach to practising sport skills. One way to help is to consider a skill's level of complexity and organisation. Complexity refers to the number of parts to the skill. Highly complex tasks have many component parts, and examples may include a figure-skating routine, the Olympic weightlifting disciplines and the pole vault. Low-complexity skills have relatively fewer component parts, and examples include shooting, the bench press and darts. Complexity does not equate to difficulty. It still requires much practice and expertise, for example, to become an elite shooter or dart thrower. Organisation refers to the relationships among a skill's component parts. In skills with a high degree of organisation, the component parts are interdependent. The way one component is performed is influenced by the way other parts are executed, and examples may include a volleyball spike, javelin throw and tennis serve. In skills with low levels of organisation the component parts are relatively independent of each other and examples may include a gymnastics, figure skating, or dance routine. It may be preferable to practise the whole skill if it has high levels of organisation and a low degree of complexity. In contrast, a part approach may be the practice method of choice for skills that are low in organisation but high in complexity.

Coaches may implement part practice in different ways and can select one of a number of strategies to suit the skill being developed. As a first example, fractionalisation involves identifying subtasks normally executed together and practising them separately before combining them again (e.g. practising the strumming and the fretting aspects of guitar playing). Evidence does exist, however, that both fractionalisation and a whole practice strategy is effective for bimanual coordination tasks. As a second example, some tasks, such as gymnastics routines, are a series of discrete skills, each of which may be practised separately. For these skills, a progressive part or segmentation learning method is suitable and involves athletes practising each skill separately and then starting to chain them together. A guitar player may learn the chorus of a song before practising the separate verses. As a third example, for complex skills, coaches may be able to simplify the movements (simplification) by changing the equipment, reducing task complexity, providing auditory or other guides, or reducing the speed of the movement. As athletes become proficient, task complexity is increased. Guitar players may initially use a metronome, slow a song down or begin with a simple strumming pattern before speeding up the song or using a complicated strumming pattern.

The two approaches (whole versus part) are not exclusive. Coaches often use the whole–part–whole approach. Athletes start by practising the whole skill to help them develop a mental map of the movement or to help them identify possible areas of weakness. Then they focus on specific parts before practising the whole skill again. Doing so allows athletes to practise individual skills and learn how the different parts of the movements relate to each other.

MENTAL PRACTICE

As discussed in Chapter 7, imagery involves the mental creation of images from memory rather than physical stimuli. There are a vast number of studies revealing that imagery increases skill-learning. Although athletes vary in their imagery abilities, they can still benefit from engaging in the strategy. Coaches may help their charges by identifying ways for athletes to use the technique before, during and after training or competition. Readers may find details in Chapter 7 helpful.

The information just discussed may assist Coach Sweets to think about how he can structure training sessions to help athletes gain the most from their skill practice. He may also find that misbehaviour among the players decreases because they are focused on the task at hand. Player management was another area where Lance believed he could improve, given the difficulties he had with Jack and Seeley. During his training as a psychologist, Lance had been exposed to research on behaviour change, and one topic that would help him is operant conditioning, or the principle that people learn from the consequences of their actions.

LEARNING FROM THE CONSEQUENCES

In the early twentieth century, a psychology student named Edward Thorndike studied how quickly a cat could learn to press a lever to open a door so it could get out of a box and obtain food. He proposed the law of effect: behaviours followed by positive consequences will be more likely to reoccur, whereas those followed by negative consequences will be less likely to happen again. Although Thorndike's work seems unrelated to sport, his discovery triggered a large line of research that provides a platform for understanding how to change human behaviour. Later, Burrhus Frederic Skinner expanded Thorndike's and others' work, becoming a highly influential psychologist and helping to develop the theory of operant conditioning. Sport psychologists and coaches have used operant conditioning principles to help athletes modify behaviour and learn a range of physical, social and psychological skills.

According to operant conditioning, behaviour is influenced by its consequences (Holt *et al.* 2012). For example, a basketball player is likely to adhere to a consistent behavioural pre-shot routine if associated with increased free-throw performance. Although Skinner and other behaviourists do not deny the existence of feelings and thoughts, they argue these are not needed to understand learning and behaviour. Concepts such as self-confidence or attention are not needed to explain the above basketball player's adherence to a pre-shot routine. Instead, increased adherence is the result of positive consequences (improved performance). Three aspects of operant conditioning include antecedents, behaviour and consequences. To understand operant conditioning, it is helpful to start with the consequences.

CONSEQUENCES

There are two dimensions to consequences. They can: (a) be positive or negative; and (b) result in something being given to or taken away from the person. These two dimensions lead to the following types of consequences:

- *Positive reinforcement*: The frequency of a behaviour increases because athletes experience positive consequences. For example, athletes praised for being early to training or who get extra instruction may continue turning up before the scheduled start time.
- *Negative reinforcement*: The frequency of a behaviour increases because negative consequences are removed. For example, athletes may turn up early for training because they avoid experiencing the coach's criticisms for being late.
- *Extinction*: The frequency of a behaviour decreases, and it eventually stops occurring, because it is no longer connected with reinforcement. For example, athletes may stop being early for training because the coach no longer interacts with them until training starts or chastises them for being late.
- *Positive punishment*: The frequency of a behaviour decreases because it leads to negative consequences. For example, athletes may avoid being late to training (and so arrive on time or early) because being late results in criticism from the coach.
- *Negative punishment*: The frequency of a behaviour decreases because positive consequences are removed. For example, athletes may stop being early for training because they receive no praise or extra instruction.

To help remember the differences among the types of consequences it is useful to appreciate that reinforcement, regardless of whether it is positive or negative, increases the frequency of behaviour. Punishment, again regardless of whether it is positive or negative, decreases the frequency of behaviour. Also, there is a subtle difference between extinction and negative punishment. In extinction there is no connection between the behaviour and the reinforcement: the athlete does not receive the reinforcement under any condition. In negative punishment, however, the valued consequence is removed.

REINFORCEMENT SCHEDULES

Although Coach Sweets might be aware of some reinforcements and punishments he could use with the players, to use them effectively he also needs to consider how often to apply them. Reinforcement schedules refer to the patterns and frequencies of reinforcement, and they are associated with different rates of learning. When using continuous reinforcement schedules, coaches reinforce the behaviour each time it occurs. Almost every time a soccer team gets the ball into the opposition's goal, a point is added to their score. With intermittent or partial reinforcement, only a proportion of the behaviour's occurrences are reinforced (many people buy lottery tickets each week, but only occasionally win a prize). Partial reinforcement may be undertaken according to ratio or interval schedules. With ratio schedules a specific percentage of occurrences are reinforced (a coach might offer feedback after every tenth attempt at a skill). With interval schedules, there is a specified length of time between reinforcement (a coach might wait for five minutes before offering feedback).

Partial reinforcement schedules may also be either fixed or variable. With a fixed schedule, reinforcement is offered after a particular number of the behaviour's occurrences or time period. The coach might always wait five minutes or for each tenth attempt before offering feedback. On a variable schedule, the time period waited or number of the behaviour's occurrences varies randomly around an average.

Continuous reinforcement leads to quicker learning over its partial counterpart, perhaps because it is easier to perceive the behaviour–consequence connection. Behaviour, however, extinguishes more rapidly after a continuous regime is halted compared with a partial schedule, probably because it is easier to perceive that the connection no longer exists. Behaviour is learned more slowly on partial rather than continuous reinforcement schedules, but is also more resistant to extinction (especially if the schedules are variable). Similarly, ratio schedules are associated with quicker learning than interval ones, and fixed regimes outperform variable systems. Based on these observations, one way that coaches can implement reinforcement may be to initially adopt continuous reinforcement schedules until behaviour change has been established and then gradually shift to variable schedules.

ANTECEDENTS

An antecedent or discriminative stimulus is an event, object, person or situation that signals that a specific behaviour will result in certain consequences. For example, the presence of stern referees or officials signals to athletes that they will be penalised for engaging in unsporting behaviour. Much behaviour in sport is influenced by discriminative stimuli. For example, successful skill execution often relies on athletes learning to identify and interpret environmental cues and then produce the correct response to achieve their goal. When antecedents are influential in regulating behaviour, the action is said to have come under stimulus control. As an illustration of stimulus control, highly skilled athletes are able to respond automatically without conscious thought to environmental discriminative cues.

The watchful gaze of a referee may be enough for some rugby league players to avoid engaging in foul play, illustrating operant generalisation. In operant generalisation a behaviour (obeying the rules) occurs to a new antecedent (referee) that was similar to the original one. In contrast, other players may test each referee they encounter to assess how much bending of the rules they can achieve (operant discrimination). In operant discrimination a specific behaviour will occur with one antecedent stimulus but not to another, albeit similar, one.

APPLICATION OF OPERANT CONDITIONING

Shaping, or the method of successive approximation, involves the reinforcing of successive approximations of a final behaviour and can speed up the learning process. For example, a cricket batter might not be adjusting her feet placement enough so that she can play shots correctly off the front foot. With shaping a coach might reinforce the athlete as she shows increased flexibility to adjust her foot placement and withhold reinforcement when she regresses until only correct adjustment is demonstrated.

Chaining may be used to develop a sequence of behaviours by reinforcing each one with the chance to perform the next action. In a dance routine, for example, an instructor might allow the athletes to start working on the next component of the routine once they have reach a level of proficiency in the previous one.

Self-regulation involves athletes applying the principles of operant conditioning to change and modify their own behaviour. The following example illustrates how athletes might engage in self-regulation.

- *Specify the behaviour to be changed.* A golfer may realise his practice sessions are too haphazard and lack sufficient direction for him to obtain optimal benefits. As a result he identifies a behavioural target to achieve, such as '80 per cent of the time spent in skills training will be focused on improving those shots at which I am currently poor'.
- *Collect baseline data.* The golfer then starts to keep a record of how he spends his skills training time and of the shots he played in each competition round. Over time he starts to identify that he tends to spend large portions of his skills training focused on his favourite shots and the ones that were going well in his previous competition.
- *Identify the antecedents and consequences.* Regarding antecedents, the golfer realises that he does not spend enough time planning his skills training or reviewing his previous competition rounds to identify his current strengths and weaknesses. With respect to consequences, he also notices that he enters rounds hoping that he will avoid having to play shots for which he lacks confidence. Such thoughts are associated with increased anxiety and beliefs about being underprepared.
- *Develop a plan to modify the antecedents and consequences.* To alter the antecedents, the golfer structures his day so that before he leaves his house to go to training he reviews his last several rounds and recent training records so he can produce a written plan for his next skill session. He also keeps a record of his skills training

during the practice session. To alter the consequences the golfer institutes a token economy. He places Monopoly money in a jar after each skills training session in which he spends at least 80 per cent of the time focused on his weakest shots. The money represents what he will allow himself to spend on his other passions. As well as this token economy, the golfer keeps a record of his training and competitive performance over time, along with his anxiety levels, negative thoughts and confidence prior to competitive rounds.

- *Implement the programme and continue keeping records.* Self-regulation programmes sometimes need to be modified once implemented because they are not always tailored well enough to athletes' needs. Also, athletes and their circumstances change. Maybe, for example, the golfer realises that he is not putting enough Monopoly money in the jar to keep him motivated, and he increases the amount.

The above example contains the typical elements involved in a self-regulation programme: planning, objective setting, design, implementation and evaluation. The example also reveals that effective programmes are tailored to the athletes' needs and circumstances.

GUIDELINES WHEN USING OPERANT CONDITIONING

- *Identify effective reinforcement.* In sport, coaches can reinforce athletes using social gestures, such as praise, smiles and applause, and using sport-related consequences, such as extra game time, practice opportunities, or instruction. Creativity and discernment may help in some circumstances because athletes vary in what they perceive as being reinforcement. Some athletes may appreciate a pat on the back, whereas others may not. Coaches who get to know their athletes' likes and dislikes will likely be able to identify effective reinforcement.
- *Be systematic in using reinforcement.* Adopting a systematic approach helps ensure that coaches use reinforcement effectively rather than haphazardly. For example, coaches who praise athletes for everything may find that their players become desensitised and eventually ignore their words of encouragement. As suggested

above, a useful strategy is to reinforce frequently when athletes are first learning a skill or attempting to modify their behaviour, and then less often over time as athletes become proficient at the movement or action. In addition, athletes may find successful skill execution satisfying in itself, so the need to provide additional reinforcement may become superfluous.

- *Reinforce a variety of behaviours.* Coaches can use operant conditioning principles to assist a variety of behavioural changes, not just those related to skill acquisition. Reinforcing effort, for example, may help athletes persevere when they do not achieve their goals or perform below expectations. Coaches may also reinforce prosocial behaviours, along with instances of teamwork and cooperation.

- *Reinforce immediately where possible.* Research has generally revealed that immediate reinforcement has a stronger effect than when delayed. People, however, can imagine future events and can remember their behaviour, so delayed reinforcement may still be effective when it is not possible to do so immediately.

- *Use punishment sparingly.* Punishment is effective at decreasing the frequency of behaviour, but does so through fear (Smith 2010). Excessive punishment may breed a fear of failure and hesitancy in athletes. Fear of failure may be associated with anxiety, making mistakes and poor performance. Punishment may also weaken the coach–athlete relationship.

FEEDBACK

Feedback is a third topic that Coach Sweets learned about during his psychologist training that he can apply to his coaching. Feedback involves the information that results from movement. For example, spectators roaring in delight as a home-town favourite attains a new world record at the Olympics is one type of feedback, as is internal sensory information golfers feel when they produce the perfect shot. There are several types of feedback, and examples include:

- *Intrinsic feedback* refers to the information that normally occurs as a consequence of movement and can arise from either outside or inside the athlete's body. Typically, athletes attain intrinsic feedback without assistance. For example, the pole vaulter can see the bar remaining still and can feel the air being expelled from her chest as she hits the mat.

- *Extrinsic feedback* refers to information from an outside source that is not a consequence of the movement, such as that provided by a coach or spectator. Extrinsic feedback can be classified as the knowledge of results or the knowledge of performance.
- *Knowledge of results* informs performers about their movement in relation to their intended goal, such as telling a lawn bowler the shot was half a metre short of the jack. Although often redundant in many situations, knowledge of results can assist athletes in many situations, such as novices who may not know how to interpret their intrinsic feedback.
- *Knowledge of performance* addresses information about the quality of movement, such as the rhythm, efficiency or aesthetic appeal. For example, a dance sport instructor may inform the couple their routine flowed well with one move melding seamlessly into the next.
- *Kinematic feedback* provides information about the distance, speed, acceleration, or other movement dimensions of a skill execution.

Coaches provide extrinsic feedback for several purposes with one of the most common reasons being to inform athletes about how they might improve. They also provide feedback to motivate athletes to persist and maintain or increase their efforts to attain their goals. Changing behaviour is another reason for providing feedback, such as informing athletes how their actions affect those around them (e.g. informing Seeley above that his words and actions upset Angela and his treatment of her may lead her to leave the team). To achieve these aims, coaches may benefit from considering the following issues (Magill, 2011; Schmidt and Wrisberg, 2008).

PROVIDING EXTRINSIC FEEDBACK

Extrinsic feedback may not be needed in each situation. As a general rule of thumb, there is a greater need for coaches to provide extrinsic feedback for complex skills and inexperienced athletes, compared with simple tasks and experienced performers. Self-aware talented athletes, however, may not gain additional information from extrinsic feedback. In addition, providing information after every attempt may lead to extrinsic feedback dependency in novice athletes and could inhibit their learning. Identifying the purpose of supplying extrinsic feedback can help coaches decide if doing so will be useful. For example, providing feedback to inexperienced athletes might help them develop a cognitive map of the skill they are learning. Feedback may also assist them to become aware of the relevant intrinsic cues available which they can use to evaluate their own performance.

Once having identified the reason for giving extrinsic feedback, coaches then face the decision about what information to deliver. For instance, information about features that athletes can control provides them with ways to improve their skills, as opposed to those aspects over which they have no control. Athletes will sometimes be unaware of what is and is not controllable and may benefit when coaches inform them of this difference. Furthermore, research, perhaps unsurprisingly, reveals that feedback that includes both information about the movement and strategies for improving the skill is more helpful than just describing the action.

Considering the stages of learning discussed earlier may help coaches make decisions about what feedback to deliver. When first learning a movement, athletes benefit from feedback about the fundamental aspects of the skill. In cricket batting, for example, such information might include the positioning of the head and feet and the alignment of the bat in relation to the front leg for certain shots. Once learners are proficient and consistent in reproducing the fundamental aspects of a movement, then feedback about other aspects may help them adapt the skill to suit different circumstances. For example, feedback about how much force used to hit the ball and the angle of the bat may help cricketers control where they direct the ball to avoid fieldsmen.

To avoid overloading athletes with too much feedback, coaches might provide summary feedback in which information about each attempt is delivered after a specified number of trials (possibly along with strategies for improvement). There is research suggesting that, compared with feedback provided after every attempt, summary information leads to poorer performance within a single practice, but better retention of learning at a later testing session. Learners may become dependent on continuous feedback, whereas summary information may encourage them to engage in self-evaluation which is then compared with the summary material the coach provides.

CONCLUSION

The material presented above may help Coach Sweets with the two issues he expressed to Daisy. The sections on stages of learning, practice organisation and provision of feedback may help him structure training so that the players engage in focused, progressive and deliberate skill development. In addition, such focused behaviour may reduce the player management difficulties Lance experienced in the first training session. The material on operant conditioning may also help him to manage misbehaviour as well as promote prosocial behaviour among the team.

More generally, the material covered in this chapter, along with the two previous ones, has provided some insight into the contributions psychologists can make to enhancing athletes' experiences in sport. Chapter 7 revealed ways in which sport psychologists can help individual athletes improve their mental skills. Chapter 6 demonstrated how practitioners can assist groups to function effectively. This chapter has focused on how psychologists may assist coaches with physical skill development. As discussed at the start of the book, sport psychology is an applied science focused on helping people improve themselves, enhance their performance and gain more enjoyment, satisfaction and happiness from an activity that is strongly valued in society.

REFERENCES

Ericsson, K. A. (2007). Deliberate practice and the modifiability of body and mind: Toward a science of the structure and acquisition of expert and elite performance. *International Journal of Sport Psychology, 38,* 4–34.

Fitts, P. M. and Posner, M. I. (1967). *Human performance.* Belmont, CA: Brooks/ Cole.

Holt, N., Bremner, A., Sutherland, E., Vliek, M., Passer, M. and Smith, R. (2012). *Psychology: The science of mind and behaviour* (2nd ed.). Maidenhead, Berkshire: McGraw-Hill.

Magill, R. A. (2011). *Motor learning: Concepts and applications* (9th ed.). New York: McGraw-Hill.

Schmidt, R. A. and Wrisberg, C. A. (2008). *Motor learning and performance: A situation-based learning approach* (4th ed.). Champaign, IL: Human Kinetics.

Smith, R. E. (2010). A positive approach to coaching effectiveness and performance enhancement. In J. M. Williams (Ed.), *Applied sport psychology: Personal growth to peak performance* (6th ed., pp. 42–58). New York: McGraw-Hill.

GLOSSARY

Achievement motivation—An individual's drive to strive for success, to overcome failure and obstacles and to experience pride in goal attainment.

Agreeableness—A five-factor model dimension referring to the extent a person is cooperative and compassionate towards others.

Amotivation—The lack of motivation towards an activity.

Anxiety—The perception of a threat, accompanied by worry, nervousness and apprehension.

Arousal—An athlete's level of mental, physical and behavioural activity or excitation in the body that ranges from low to high and varies on a moment-by-moment basis.

Athlete Apperception Test—A projective test in which athletes are given illustrations of athletes in ambiguous sporting situations.

Attribution—An athlete's perceived cause of an event.

Attribution bias—People tend to attribute positive events to internal causes and negative events to external causes.

Audience—The presence of other people, who are attending to, and evaluating, task performance.

Audience effects—The influence that the presence of an audience has on individuals' psychological states, behaviours and performances.

Behavioural observations—An approach to collecting information by observing athletes in the sporting context.

Biofeedback—Interventions in which people learn to monitor and control bodily functions.

Biological approach—An approach to explaining the influences that genes and physiological factors have on personality.

Blocked practice—A type of practice where athletes focus on one skill variation.

Case study—An in-depth examination of a single person, event or organisation.

Chaining—A skill-learning strategy used to develop a sequence of behaviours by reinforcing each one with the chance to perform the next action.

Coaching Behaviour Assessment System—A behaviour observation tool designed to help people collect information about the behaviour of coaches.

Coactive teams—Individuals compete side-by-side with limited interaction (e.g. canoeists).

Cognitive and behavioural strategies—The psychological skills and strategies athletes use when competing.

Cognitive anxiety—The mental aspects of anxiety: the worries, doubts and concerns athletes have about performance or other issues and events.

Cohesion—The degree to which a group of athletes work together in pursuit of their goals and achieve member satisfaction.

Cohort study (longitudinal study)—Research in which investigators follow a group of people over time, measuring variables on multiple occasions.

Collective efficacy—A group's shared belief in its combined resources to undertake actions to achieve a task.

Competition—A social process in which rewards are distributed unequally based on people's performance in comparison to others participating in the same event.

Competition plan—A plan or routine athletes have for structuring both their build-up to an event and how they intend to perform during a contest.

Competitive State Anxiety Inventory-2—A questionnaire measuring athletes' cognitive anxiety, somatic anxiety and self-confidence.

Complexity (skill-learning)—Refers to the number of parts to a skill. Highly complex skills have many parts.

Confidence—Individuals' beliefs that they have the resources to achieve success.

Conscientiousness—A five-factor model dimension referring to the degree an individual is organised, diligent and scrupulous.

Contextual interference—The impairment of learning that results from practising variations of a skill in the same session.

Continuous reinforcement schedule—Behaviour is reinforced after every occurrence.

Cross-sectional study—Research in which investigators measure variables in a group people on one occasion.

Defence mechanism—A strategy (often subconscious) that people use to deny, change or modify reality to cope with anxiety.

Desire to achieve success—Within Atkinson's theory, a personality factor reflecting how much a person focuses on the positive consequences of achieving a goal.

Desire to avoid failure—Within Atkinson's theory, a personality factor reflecting how much a person focuses on the negative consequences of failing to achieve a goal.

Discriminative stimuli—An event, object, person or situation that signals that a specific behaviour will result in certain consequences.

Distributed practice—(a) Athletes focus on multiple skill variations in a session and the drill order may be random; or (b) within a session there are relatively long rests between skill attempts.

Drive for muscularity—A person's desire to build muscle.

Ego—According to Freud's theory, the aspect of our personality that attempts to control the impulses of the id.

Ego orientation—A goal orientation in which athletes define success through demonstrating superior ability over others.

Eros—Within Freud's theory, the drive for life, love and sex.

Exercise psychology—The study of the interactions among people's thoughts, feelings, behaviours and environments in exercise-related settings.

Experiment—A type of research study in which investigators manipulate one factor (independent variable) to examine its influence on another factor (dependent variable).

External imagery—An imagery perspective that refers to when athletes imagine themselves performing as if they were viewing themselves on a television.

External regulation—When athletes participate in a sport for rewards imposed by externally defined goals.

Extinction—The frequency of a behaviour decreases, and it eventually stops occurring, because it is no longer connected with reinforcement.

Extraversion—A personality characteristic in which individuals like to be the centre of attention, prefer to be in social situations and focus less on themselves and more on external events and stimuli.

Extrinsic feedback—Feedback from an outside source that is not a consequence of the movement, such as that provided by a coach or spectator.

Extrinsic motivation—The drive to participate in an activity for a tangible or intangible reward not inherent to the task.

Feedback—Information about an athlete's performance of a task, often given as a basis for improvement.

Five-factor model—A trait personality theory that suggests that the various personality traits can be categorised within five dimensions: extraversion, agreeableness, conscientiousness, neuroticism and openness to experience.

Fixed reinforcement schedule—Reinforcement is offered after a particular number of a behaviour's occurrences or time period.

Fractionalisation—A part practice strategy for skills in which different subtasks are performed simultaneously. Each subtask is practised separately before being practised together.

Goal—A specific standard of performance to be reached or outcome to be secured.

Goal involvement—The goals that athletes are focused on in a specific situation at a particular time.

Goal-setting—An intervention in which athletes decide what goals they want to achieve, how they can achieve those targets and the time by which they will have completed them.

Group—Two or more individuals who interact, typically with a common goal.

Groupthink—A type of interaction displayed by group members when trying to minimise conflict and reach a consensus without testing and evaluating ideas.

Home advantage—Refers to the tendency for athletes and teams to obtain better results when playing at home rather than away.

'Hot hand' effect—The notion that after a run of successes a player is more likely to succeed with their next play or game than if they had experienced a series of failures.

Humanistic approach—An approach to personality in which people are viewed as basically good and striving for personal fulfilment.

Hypothesis—A researcher's expected outcome of a study.

Iceberg profile—Morgan's mental health model in which athletes report higher vigour but lower depression, anger, fatigue, confusion and tension compared with the general population.

Id—According to Freud's theory, the aspect of our personality that attempts to satisfy our instinctual drives.

Ideal Performance State—The profile of mental and physical states that allow athletes to perform to their potential.

Identified regulation—Athletes participate in a sport because they identify with the activity's purpose and values.

Imagery—A mental process involving multisensory experiences in the absence of actual perception.

Independent team—Individuals compete separately (e.g. gymnasts).

Integrated regulation—When athletes participate in a sport because doing so is coherent with their life goals, lifestyle and sense of identity.

Interactive team—Individuals continuously interact with each other throughout the contest (e.g. soccer, volleyball)

Intermittent (or partial) reinforcement schedule—Only a proportion of an action's occurrences are reinforced.

Internal imagery—An imagery perspective that refers to when athletes imagine themselves performing as if they were looking through their own eyes.

Inter-rater reliability—The degree to which different observers score the same behaviour similarly.

Interval reinforcement schedule—There is a specified length of time between reinforcement.

Intra–rater reliability—The degree to which a person scores the same behaviour similarly over time.

Intrinsic feedback—Feedback that normally occurs as a consequence of movement and can arise from either outside or inside the athlete's body.

Intrinsic motivation—The drive to participate in an activity for the satisfactions gained inherent to the task.

Introjected regulation—When athletes control their own participation through reward and punishment.

Introversion—A personality characteristic in which individuals are less outgoing, focus more on their own thoughts and feelings and prefer small social groups.

Kinaesthetic sense—The feeling of movement.

Kinematic feedback—Provides information about the distance, speed, acceleration, or other movement dimensions of a skill execution.

Kinematics—The study of the spatial and temporal characteristics of motion (e.g. displacement, velocity).

Kinesiology—The study of human movement.

Kinetics—The study of the forces that cause, facilitate, change or inhibit motion of a body (e.g. friction, gravity).

Knowledge of performance—Feedback about the quality of a movement, such as the rhythm, efficiency or aesthetic appeal.

Knowledge of results—Feedback that informs performers about their movements in relation to their intended goals.

Law of effect—Behaviours followed by positive consequences are more likely to reoccur, whereas those followed by negative repercussions are less likely to transpire again.

Leader—Someone who influences a team or player towards goal achievement.

Learned helplessness—The belief that one has no control over negative events.

Life skills—Cognitive, emotional, social and behavioural abilities allowing people to cope with the demands of everyday life.

Locus of causality—The perceived location of an event's cause; either internal or external to an athlete.

Longitudinal study (cohort study)—Research in which investigators follow a group of people over time, measuring variables on multiple occasions.

Massed practice—In massed practice the amount of rest between skill attempts is short or non-existent.

Mastery experience—A self-efficacy source that derives from having previously attempted the task.

Mental health model—Morgan's 'iceberg profile' in which athletes report higher vigour but lower depression, anger, fatigue, confusion and tension compared with the general population.

Meta-analysis—A study in which investigators use statistical procedures to combine the results from existing research to determine the relationship between two variables.

Method of successive approximation (or shaping)—In skill-learning, the reinforcing of successive approximations of a final behaviour until only the desired action is reinforced.

Modelling—Within social learning theory, modelling involves learning by watching how other people act and then imitating them.

Moderator—A variable that influences the strength of a relationship between two other variables.

Mood states—Right-now feelings that change from moment to moment.

Motivation—The force that impels us to achieve a goal and includes the direction and intensity of an athlete's behaviour.

Motivational climate—Describes the collection of goals and values emphasised by significant others in an athlete's social environment.

Negative punishment—The frequency of a behaviour decreases because positive consequences are removed.

Negative reinforcement—The frequency of a behaviour increases because negative consequences are removed.

NEO Personality Inventory–Revised—A standardised questionnaire measuring each dimension of the five-factor model.

Neuroticism—A personality characteristic associated with being moody, anxious, rigid, touchy, restless, aggressive and a tendency to experience psychological distress.

Objective competitive situation—The actual competitive situation in which an athlete has to compete.

Openness to experience—A five-factor model dimension referring to an appreciation for the arts, emotions, adventures, unusual ideas, imagination, curiosity and various experiences.

Operant conditioning—A theory that explains how behaviour's consequences determine the future frequency of the action.

Operant discrimination—Occurs when behaviour occurs with one antecedent stimulus but not with another (even if similar).

Operant generalisation—When behaviours occur after new discriminative stimuli that are similar to the original one.

Organisation (skill-learning)—Refers to the relationships among the components of a skill. Components are interdependent in highly organised skills.

Outcome goals (in goal-setting)—A standard of achievement based on a social comparison (e.g. winning a competition).

Overlearning—Athletes continue to practise a skill after achieving a specified standard of proficiency.

Partial (or intermittent) reinforcement schedule—Only a proportion of an action's occurrences are reinforced.

Participation motivation—The reasons athletes give for playing a sport.

Perceived competence—The perceptions people have about their skill levels at a task.

Perfectionism—A trait or tendency to strive for flawlessness, the setting of overly high standards and refusal to accept less than perfection, accompanied by excessive critical self-evaluation and concern for others' approval.

Performance approach goal—Goals that reflect athletes' desires to do well relative to others (people are motivated to play to win).

Performance avoidance goal—Goals that reflect athletes' desires to avoid doing poorly compared with others (people play to avoid losing).

Performance goal (in goal-setting)—A goal identifying a standard of achievement independent of other people (e.g. running 100 metres in less than 10 seconds).

Personality—The blend of characteristics (thoughts, feelings and behaviours) that make individuals unique and consistent over time.

Person-centred therapy—An approach to therapy in which psychologists help clients develop self-awareness and solutions to their issues within a supportive relationship.

Positive punishment—The frequency of a behaviour decreases because it leads to negative consequences.

Positive reinforcement—The frequency of a behaviour increases when followed by positive consequences.

Pre-performance routine—An established and practised set of thought processes and behaviours athletes carry out before performing self-paced tasks.

Process goal (in goal-setting)—Details behaviours that athletes will focus on during performance.

Profile of Mood States—A standardised questionnaire that measures a person's moods, including anger, depression, confusion, fatigue and tension.

Progressive part practice—A part practice strategy for tasks consisting of a series of sub-movements. Athletes practice each component of a task before adding the next movement to the chain.

Projective test—A personality measuring tool in which people are asked to respond to ambiguous stimuli such as pictures or inkblots.

Psychodynamic theory—A view that explains personality in terms of the interplay among the conscious beliefs, unconscious forces and environment.

Psychological momentum—A change (typically triggered by an event) in an athlete's thoughts, feelings, physical states or behaviour that influences performance or outcomes.

Psychological skills training programmes—An intervention package in which sport psychologists help athletes use psychological strategies to develop characteristics associated with enhanced performance.

Psychology—The study of the interactions among people's or animal's thoughts, feelings, behaviour and environments.

Qualitative study—Research in which words, texts, video, sounds, etc., form the basis of the data collected.

Quantitative study—Research in which numbers form the basis of the data collected.

Ratio reinforcement schedule—A specific percentage of an action's occurrences are reinforced.

Reactive teams—Individuals respond to their teammates' actions, but not always at the same time (e.g. the softball catcher, pitcher, fielder and person holding base).

Refocusing plan—Strategies athletes use when they need to regain control and their focus during a competitive event.

Reliability—The extent to which measures are consistent over time, across items (in a questionnaire), or across people.

Research—Systematic investigation into some phenomenon of interest to create knowledge, establish facts and reach new conclusions.

Ringelmann effect—As group size increases, individual members become less productive.

Science—A way of learning about the world through systematic and controlled observation and experience.

Scientific method—A four-stage process underpinning science, consisting of: (a) developing a question; (b) stating a hypothesis; (c) collecting data; and (d) analysing results.

Scientist-practitioner model—A model of applied sport psychology practitioner training in which students are given a grounding in the scientific method so that science and practice inform and guide each other.

Self-confidence—Athletes' perceptions about their abilities to achieve success.

Self-efficacy—Athletes' beliefs they can execute the behaviours needed to produce desired outcomes.

Self-handicapping—A strategy that involves the reduction of effort to avoid failure from reflecting poorly on oneself. It may also involve the creation or identification of obstacles in anticipation of poor performance.

Self-regulation—Involves individuals applying the principles of operant conditioning to modify their own behaviour. The typical steps involve specifying the behaviour to be changed, collecting baseline data, identifying the antecedents and consequences, developing and implementing a plan to modify the antecedents and consequences, and keeping records.

Self-talk—Statements individuals say to themselves, either out loud or in their minds.

Shaping (or method of successive approximation)—In skill-learning, the reinforcing of successive approximations of a final behaviour until only the desired action is reinforced.

Simplification (skill-learning)—A part practice strategy in which the complexity of a skill is reduced.

Social cognitive approach—An approach that explains personality in terms of the ways people organise information, make decisions and evaluate consequences.

Social cohesion—Refers to the degree that individuals like being part of a group and enjoy each other's company.

Social facilitation—Refers to the tendency for an audience to elicit the dominant response from individuals performing a task. Performance typically increases for simple and well-learned tasks. Performance typically decreases for complex and novel tasks.

Social learning theory—A theory that suggests people do not need to be rewarded and punished directly to learn suitable and unsuitable behaviour, but can learn through modelling. The theory suggests most behaviour is learned through modelling.

Social loafing—Occurs when individuals make less effort to achieve a goal when they work in groups than when alone.

Social orientation—A person's tendency to approach social situations either positively (with self-assurance and enthusiasm) or negatively (with anxiety and apprehension).

Somatic anxiety—Athletes' perceptions of their physiological arousal.

Sport confidence—Athletes' beliefs about their ability to be successful in sport.

Sport psychology—The study of the interactions among people's thoughts, feelings, behaviours and environments in sport settings.

Sport science (or sport and exercise science)—The application of scientific principles and techniques to improve sporting (and exercise) performance or experience.

Standardised questionnaire—A questionnaire that presents the same questions to test takers who respond in a uniform manner.

State anxiety—Athletes' right-now, moment-to-moment perceptions of threat and accompanying worries, nervousness and apprehension.

State self-confidence—Athletes' belief about their ability to succeed in the current situation.

States—A right-now way of behaving, thinking or feeling that may change on a moment-to-moment basis.

Stress—The perceived imbalance between the requirements of the task and the athlete's capability to meet those demands where failure to cope carries negative consequences.

Subjective competitive situation—An athlete's interpretation of the objective competitive situation.

Superego—According to Freud's theory, the aspect of our personality that attempts to internalise the values we have learned from our parents and society.

Task cohesion—Refers to the extent that a team of individuals work well together towards the achievement of, and accept, the group's goals.

Task orientation—An achievement goal orientation in which athletes define success through self-improvement.

Team cohesion—The propensity of a sports team to stay together in the striving for their objectives and athlete satisfaction.

Thantos—Within Freud's theory, the drive for death and aggression.

Thematic Apperception Test—A projective test in which people are given black and white illustrations of people in ambiguous situations.

Theory—A set of related facts that explains a phenomenon of interest.

Trait—Relatively consistent and enduring aspect of personality and behaviour.

Trait anxiety—Individuals' predispositions to perceive events or situations as threatening and to respond with high levels of anxiety.

Trait approach—An approach that explains personality in terms of traits.

Trait competitiveness—A person's tendency to compete against others in an activity.

Trait self-confidence—Athletes' general perception regarding their abilities to achieve success.

Transformational leaders—Charismatic individuals who inspire followers to extraordinary outcomes through idealised influence, inspirational motivation, intellectual stimulation and individualised consideration.

Validity—The degree to which psychological measurement tools assess what they are designed to measure.

Variable reinforcement schedule—The time period or number of the behaviour's occurrences between reinforcements varies randomly around an average.

Verbal persuasion—A self-efficacy source that involves athletes being told they can perform a task.

Vicarious experience—A self-efficacy source involving athletes watching models perform a task.

INDEX